DATE DUE

9-15-02			
MY 28 '03			
JY 31 '03			
AG 28 '03			
NO 19 '04			

976.7803
Be

Bennett, Martha Cash
Home by suppertime

Home By Suppertime

Home By Suppertime

by

Martha Cash Bennett

SWEET WATERMELON BOOKS
Martha Bennett
302 Mayhaw
P.O. Box 316
Taylorsville MS 39168

Illustrations by Jill Sloan Seals

Edited by Patti Robey

Cover design by Betty Little

Calligraphy by Betty Hester

Introduction by J. Paul Du Bois

Epilogue by Kay Cash Sloan

Library of Congress Catalog No. 91-075172

ISBN 0-9630366-0-2

Typesetting and layout by Little Printing Service
Mize, Mississippi

Printing and binding by Walsworth Publishing Company
Marceline, Missouri

This book is dedicated to
Mama and Daddy and
our family.

I hope you enjoy the book!
— Martha Cash Bennett —

TABLE OF CONTENTS

INTRODUCTION

If you are like me, you may have decided to read the introduction before you buy this book. Well, I'll just say this: If you're looking for a good book on sports, maybe the thrill of victory and the agony of defeat, this ain't the book. If you're looking for a good, hot romance novel that sizzles on every page, move on to another section of this store. If you're looking for a good religious book, written by one of those billious, stand-side-ways-and-look-holy-preacher-types, look elsewhere, my friend; this ain't what you're looking for.

But if you're looking for some good wholesome fun, with a belly-laugh or two on every page, this is the book!

I saw Martha a few months ago, when we were having one of those "what-ever-happened-to-so-and-so" class reunions in our hometown in southern Missouri. She told me then that she was writing this book, an expansion of her *Home by Suppertime* vignettes which appear in newspapers in several states. I've been reading her column for some years now, and I can say that when I read one I'm just like the firefly that backed into a fan; just delighted! Martha can really turn a phrase, and I think you'll like the way she turns 'em.

Even as a small, pudgy child Martha was funny. She used to come to my Daddy's store and recite "The Crooked Mouth Family," a dramatic reading she made even more dramatic by her Ozark drawl and facial contortions (see p. 23). My dad said, "That girl's smart." Well, she was, and IS! She became a school teacher in Missouri, which is no mean accomplishment in itself. And then she became a writer, without ever being involved in any kind of scandal or entering politics!

You'll enjoy Martha's unique style. The most delightful thing about her, however, is her "Ozark twang." It is so typical of "Ozarkese" speech that a total stranger in London, England, upon over-hearing Martha talking a mile a minute right there at the Palace gates, approached her and asked "Would you be from the Ozark mountains of southern Missouri"? (see p. 141). And she "confessed to the fault." I swear, when Martha talks even E.F. Hutton would listen!

But while the reader won't be able to hear the "Ozarkese" in these stories, one can *almost* hear it—and feel a part of what we experienced during the waning days of the Great Depression years in our hometown. You'll learn from reading *Home By Suppertime* what life was like in a small town and a big family—in Oregon County, Missouri, where men were men and women were women, and the difference was deliberate!

When you have finished the reading of this book, dear friend, you'll have the feeling that you've just had a good dose of "wholesome." Have fun (and pass the book on to a friend.)

—J. Paul Du Bois
Arlington, Texas (1991)

Chapter 1

THE DOG DAYS OF SUMMER

"Mad dog's a-comin'! Mad dog's a-comin'! Run! Run! Run for your life 'cause a mad dog's a-comin'!"

Since our little hill town didn't offer a whole lot in the way of entertainment during the summer school vacation, it probably was not unusual that the kids in our family looked forward to the coming of early August when the warning that mad dogs were taking over the community blasted our peace and tranquility.

Daddy considered himself to be a canine authority by reason of having hunted all his life. He patiently explained to all those who would listen that the dogs were not "mad" but just severely infested with canine roundworms, and that this infestation was what caused the running seizures we kids perversely anticipated. In those difficult days of the Great Depression few dog owners gave their animals medication to rid them of the parasites (most kids were not wormed; you could forget about worming pets) and they paid but slight attention to the frenzied antics of

1

their animals when "runnin' fits" (a colloquially used term) overcame them.

We chose to ignore Daddy's sensible explanation because the days were slow and sleepy in our part of the world and fear of being bitten by a dog with rabies (*our* diagnosis of the dog's affliction) did much to relieve the tedium of late summer.

As a general rule, we would have several seconds' warning before an attack. Our good friend, Stealy Jones, and his family lived higher up the hill than we did and Stealy had appointed himself sentry for the neighborhood. Being an extremely lazy child, he spent a lot of his life hidden high in the barn loft to avoid the weed pulling, corn hoeing, pig slopping, milking and other chores common to the rest of us. In all fairness to this freckle-faced Paul Revere of the Ozarks, I must say his perch in the sky afforded him ample opportunity to search the sparsely wooded fields which lay around our homes, and when he would bellow forth his hair-raising pronouncement of impending doom, "Mad dog's a-comin'...", every child within hearing distance made a wild dash for safety.

You want to talk about a bunch of kids moving around! A shrilly yelping dog, tail firmly tucked between its legs, circling our small group gave impetus to the laziest of the lazy. I always thought the slobbering creature encircled us in order to pick out the slowest runner to chase, and even Daddy's insistence that dogs could not in any way pinpoint the most lethargic member of the party never convinced me. Since I have ever tended to be slow on my feet, running toward corpulence and laziness as I do, it seemed more than likely even to my dull intellect that one day I would fall victim to the fearful bite of an afflicted animal and die in the most hideous manner known to mankind.

2

My oldest brother, Clark, was even more fearful than I of the slobbering monsters. He was greatly given to nightmares of a most horrible nature and during the summer months would often waken the entire household with hair-raising shrieks, moans, sobs and cries containing colorful reference to attacks being made on his person by these dribbling dogs of doom. (Once he even went so far as to make out a list of all those he planned to bite should it fall his lot to succumb to the dread disease. His teacher headed the list of those to be gnawed upon.)

When Stealy's warning blasted the serenity of our back yard we had a difficult decision to make. Was it closer to the house, or to the tree? Even though we didn't have a lot of time to make up our minds, we were often so scared that we'd jump up and down in the same spot for several seconds until someone lunged one way or the other, and then we'd all follow the leader. (I believe this oddity of moving up and down without going anywhere is now known as "jogging in place.")

With the choice made to go for the tree, the older kids grabbed the ropes which they had placed strategically on the lower limbs for just such a time of need. Once safely in the tree (and depending on how they felt at the moment), they would either help us younger ones to safety by assisting us in our climb, or else they just might impishly try to push us back into the path of the racing dog(s) which, as you can imagine, added a great deal to the spirit of excitement and camaraderie of the moment.

Needless to say, much wild shrieking accompanied our attempts to reach a secure harbor, far from harm's way, and the intensity of our screams often drew Mama onto the scene. Being an extremely nervous individual, she would frequently become totally undone and add to the general confusion by bursting into tears which continued until the dog(s) had "run out the fit" and collapsed, apparently lifeless, on the ground.

At that point we considered it safe to jump from the tree and would usually send a runner to let Stealy know that, thanks to his eagle eye and early warning system, we had survived yet another attack. Someone would carry food to Stealy's loft as a token of our gratitude, for gut level we all knew that one day the running dog would be thoroughly infected with the dreaded hydrophobia and we would become fatally diseased by breathing the same air as the afflicted animal. (Obviously we did not understand how rabies was spread.)

One day, when the choice had been to make for the safety of the house and we had reached what we thought to be the security of the living room, the tortured canine came right up on the porch and joined us by simply jumping through a hole in the screen door. (We nearly always lived in rented houses, and Daddy felt no compulsion to make even the most basic repairs to the property of others).

Now the dog was a good bit larger than the hole, and much additional damage was done to the screen door. Nothing was ever said about the destruction since the dog entering the house was a foxhound. (Much more leniency was permitted the hounds than was afforded us kids.)

On this occasion we were fortunate in that our house had an archway with bookcases on each side separating the living room from the dining area. We quickly tried to crawl on top of these shelves to escape the attentions of the slobbering monster which had invaded our home.

There were four of us to share the rather limited space atop the bookshelves; Anne (my oldest sister), Clark (older than I), Bert (just younger), and me. Clark, concerned about the crowded condition, conceived the selfish idea of forcing little Bert out of the way by hoisting him

4

high in the air until he was able to reach the upper frame of the archway. There Bert clung to the woodwork with terrified desperation while the yelping dog ran back and forth beneath his skinny legs. (In defense of Clark, I must tell you that Bert was the obvious choice. He was small, tough and mean as a snake!)

With my hysterical little brother screaming and swaying above my head, I was trying to achieve safety atop the haven of the bookcase. Unhappily for me, Clark, adrenal glands pumping full force, had decided to deter my efforts for self-preservation by stomping on my fingers. Anne, a fairly gentle child, came to my rescue and saved me by vowing to kick Clark's feet out from under him unless he permitted me to gain sanctuary alongside them.

I was grown before I realized this phenomenon was not what people were talking about when they referred to "the dog days of summer."

Chapter 2

99 AND 44/100% PURE

"Great God Almighty!" Daddy screamed when he spotted the foreign object. (Though not a deeply religious man, our father felt privileged to invoke heavenly assistance in times of emotional stress, which seemed to occur a lot around our house, and his explanation was that since he made the entire family attend church on a regular basis, the Lord certainly owed him something back, and you could be damned sure he intended to collect!)

"What in the name of God are you trying to do, woman, kill us all?" the shrieking continued. "These defenseless children...as God is my witness, Clair, you'll stunt their growth! Look at this, just look at this, will you please just look at this?!"

The evening meal had started out better than usual, since we were all on time for a change. Because there were so many of us, this did not happen every day, especially during summer, when our clan was free to spend time just about any way we saw fit (barring serious run-ins with the

7

law), so long as we were home by suppertime.

"Suppertime" was intangible and undefined and occurred when Daddy got home and was ready to eat. Since
he owned and operated a small grocery store in town, "The
Famous Market," his hours were flexible for he always
stayed until he was sure everyone had their grocery needs
for the night. Mama, being of the old school, earnestly
and sincerely believed God would strike us down dead,
each and every one, if we so much as put one bite of food
in our mouths before the man of the house was at the head
of the table. (Sometimes we waited...and waited...and
waited!)

It didn't take very long for us to learn to recognize the
roar of his old pickup truck, which met all the transportation needs of our family and a few of the neighbors. It
also saw service during the twice-daily delivery of groceries
to the home of anyone needing a loaf of bread or a can of
pork 'n' beans.

Daddy told a funny story about a time in his youth when
he worked as the local grocery delivery boy. One afternoon he failed to receive a response to his knock on the
customer's back door, so he just opened it and walked on
in. Imagine the surprise of both Daddy and the young lady
who was having a soak in the galvanized laundry tub,
which was used in those days for purposes of personal
cleanliness. Not knowing how to handle the situation, he
just tipped his hat, said "Thank you, ma'am," and
hurried away, taking the groceries with him. How he used
to laugh when he told the story but Mama nearly always
got mad. I've always wondered if she could have been the
bather.

We tried to beat the truck home because if we were very
late to the table, bad things could happen. One, all the
food could have been consumed by those fortunate

enough to be on time, or two, Mama might have decided the absent one was eating at a friend's home. In that case, she would throw the leftovers out the back door to the waiting dogs.

You see, at our house it was left up to each individual, after the weaning process had taken place, to be on hand for meals. (Mama was not one who embraced the theory that children needed to be cajoled into eating balanced meals at specific times of the day. Let me add at this point that Mama did not readily embrace any theory that had to do with spoiling children.)

Our daddy was a "fox huntin' man" and dearly loved his dogs, so they were as welcome to the good food Mama cooked as his kids were. Maybe more so. (Daddy was well-known in the community for his deep-seated conviction that good kids were a lot easier to come by than good fox-hounds, and at an early age we learned we were expendable.)

When we were all home the family numbered eight, and as a general rule we had a visiting child or two, so conversation around the table was not really encouraged. Daddy had a saying, "Let your vittles stop your mouth!" but if one or the other of us had experienced anything way out of the ordinary, such as being bitten by a copperhead snake, or chased home by a rabid dog, we were permitted to share it at this time.

Yes, the evening meal had started well. Conversation was being monopolized by my small brother, Bert (a not unusual occurrence). He was describing in great detail how he and Stealy Jones had spent a good part of the afternoon burying live baby chicks in the garden, using an old tea kettle as the coffin.

"That old hen was floggin' us pretty bad," he explained, "but we got as many of them babies away frum her as we could and stuffed 'em in an ole tea kettle we found at the

9

junk pile. Then we buried the whole thang in the garden and jest left the spout stickin' outa the groun'. Wonder how long they'll last without any thang to eat er drank?''

Someone in the group started to venture a guess as to the life expectancy of these young fowls now dwelling underground when we noticed that Daddy had a strange look on his face.

Since he was always first to be served (not unusual for that era), he was also first to notice that the wieners and kraut had an extremely odd and distasteful flavor this evening.

Never one for inaction, and no stickler for niceties either, Daddy spat the food out on his plate, jumped up so quickly he knocked his chair over, and ran to the stove to stare fixedly into the simmering pot which contained the remainder of the wieners and kraut. (Mama always cooked a lot because we never knew who might show up to eat with us at the last minute, and of course the dogs were wholly delighted to dispose of any leftovers. Like the rest of the family, they were not exactly finicky eaters and consumed kraut with great enthusiasm.)

Daddy picked up a wooden spoon and stirred briefly. Then he exploded!

''God help us all, this is just too much!'' he bellowed to the entire neighborhood. (Daddy was a small man, but you would not have known it from listening to him in his heavenly conversations. He sounded big.)

The object of his wrath lay on the wooden spoon which he thrust under Mama's nose. Much, much thinner for having been simmered off and on for an hour, rested the remains of a cake of Ivory soap. How it ever landed in the pot of wieners and kraut I cannot tell you. That must eternally remain a mystery, but there it was, white and slippery, with a few thin, wispy strings of home-made kraut hanging limply to one side.

Still shrieking, Daddy ran to the back door and threw the food, pot and all, into the yard where it was quickly consumed by the hounds. (Not the pot, just the wieners and kraut.)

Seeming somewhat comforted by this action, he gently collapsed into his chair, moaning softly while he slowly beat his forehead against the edge of the table. Mama cried a lot, which she tended to do at times of family crises, and conversation was slim to none. Through the silence Daddy could be heard quietly muttering to himself that God help him! he'd be lucky, damned lucky, to get any of us raised.

That was one of the few times I regretted making it home by suppertime.

Chapter 3

THE PASSING OF OLD PEPPER

At the time of the killing, Clark was about twelve, give or take a year or two. His youth, combined with an unfortunate tendency (inherited from Daddy) to be short-tempered, was his only excuse for the slaughter.

As the oldest boy in the family, Clark was responsible for seeing that the garden stayed in production. We lived on a rented place that had some shaky outbuildings and a few acres of cleared ground. Daddy felt the only way to survive raising a large family in the thirties without going totally broke was to live in the country. (Bankruptcy was a disgrace in my childhood, not the alternate life style some consider it today.)

So we grew a big garden. We kept a milk cow and had some chickens that ate the potato peelings and coffee grounds, which were all the scraps we ever had. (Incidentally, those chickens were responsible for Stealy Jones's nickname. Whenever they lacked funds to see a picture show, which was often, he and Clark would confiscate a fat hen to sell at the produce store. Stealy would take one from Mama's henhouse and Clark would steal from Mrs. Jones's flock. Somehow they felt it was less sinful that way. One night Stealy got caught, and we never let him forget it.)

Anyway, the garden, the cow, and the chickens all helped in the never-ending struggle to put enough food on the table to feed a big family and the wide assortment of visitors who tended to drop in with ever-increasing frequency, for the Depression seemed to deepen daily.

One of Clark's many chores was to plow out the garden before the weeds took over. In those days before garden tillers, he used our old white mule and a handheld plow for the job. Catching Old Pepper was often a bigger task than plowing the garden, for the stubborn beast seemed to invariably know what was going to happen, and he ran to the far end of the field as a general protest against the coming event.

On the day of the killing, the weather was hot...humid and unbearable as so many Ozark summer days tend to be...and as the chase began, it got hotter. Clark, being cursed with the family temper, was not long on patience.

Now it so happened my brother had taken a small-gauge shotgun along when he embarked upon the mule catching errand, just in case a rabbit or squirrel might present itself as an addition to our evening meal. That proved to be unfortunate! After what seemed like hours of futile chasing, Clark grew so enraged that he lost all control of his emotions. He threw the gun to his shoulder and cut down on his adversary!

Nine hundred and ninety-nine times out of a thousand such a shot would not seriously injure a tough-hided old mule, but down Old Pepper dropped, graveyard dead!

Clark was bothered. A lot. It made him sick. Since our

father tended to become extremely upset over small happenings, there was no telling how he would react to the loss of Old Pepper, and Clark began to seriously consider running away from home.

Well, in one small way luck was with him. The mule had fallen into a big ditch and was lying on the side which had sustained the gunshot wound. Ever quick thinking, Clark hit on the idea of suppressing a bit of the truth. He felt he might, just might, get away with reporting the basic fact, that the old mule was dead as a post in the ditch, without mentioning his major contribution to its method of reaching that big haystack in the sky.

At suppertime Daddy inquired as to how the plowing had gone for the day. With quivering voice, knowing gut level we were in for a traumatic evening meal, Clark related the sad story of finding Old Pepper dead in the big ditch. As I recall, he even managed to shed a few tears. Clark was pretty good at that sort of thing, having had a lot of practice down through the years.

At the end of the brief report, Daddy screamed, "Great God Almighty! I want to know, dear Lord above, I want to know what I have ever done in my life to be punished this way! I'm at the end of my rope, do you hear me? The end of my rope...and I'm through...completely and totally washed up! THIS IS IT...!!!" (Daddy adopted a very formal tone in his heavenly tirades and just grew more and more eloquent until exhaustion took over. His manner of addressing his maker was highly reminiscent of a revival preacher seeking the return of lost souls to the fold.)

The passionate conversation continued until all the heavenly hosts had been addressed, and Daddy had worn out. He sank back into his chair and rested his head on the supper table. About the only sign of life was a vein pulsating rapidly in his left temple.

15

Though he pondered deeply on the matter, Daddy never could figure out what might have caused that mule to drop dead in the prime of its life.

Clark didn't tell him for at least twenty years.

Chapter 4

SCHOOL DAYS, SCHOOL DAYS

Our little community, aptly named "Fair" by the early settlers, was located in south central Missouri, about two miles north of the Arkansas-Missouri border. It was and continues to be a "railroad town," the terminal of the Burlington-Northern Railroad (formerly Frisco) between Memphis, Tennessee and Springfield, Missouri. Men fortunate enough to be employed by the Frisco (we called it "workin' on the road"), were considered only a tiny bit shy of wealthy and thus bitterly envied by the rest of us who just barely got by. (I remember Mama saying she and Daddy made it through the first year of their marriage on less than ten dollars a week, and they both drank coffee, an almost unbelievable luxury for the time.)

The town lay at the bottom of a high hill which in any other part of the world would be considered a small mountain. At the very pinnacle of the peak stood our school, the largest edifice to learning in Oregon County. Surrounded by a large wooded area which was known to the older

17

folks as "the park," this big brick building, along with the grove of old oak trees, was impressive to little kids just embarking on their educational journey.

The school had three levels (we called them "floors"), including a basement where the furnace room, lunch room, music room, and rest rooms were located.

Can you believe we actually learned to read music in the music room? I mean the teacher drew lines and notes on the black board, explained what it all meant, and taught us to harmonize (I use the term in its very loosest sense!) while we were yet in grade school. Dear Miss McCarthy, our teacher, thought that music classes were held to teach children about music. Such a simple time!

The rest rooms, actually quite humble, seemed places of wonder to those of us not accustomed to the marvels of modern plumbing. On first entering school, I stood in awe of the porcelain fixtures for several weeks until familiarity caused me to become as blase' as my fellow students and I flushed with the best of them.

The lunch room held a lot of interest for me because of my overwhelming enjoyment of food, and lots of swapping and promises of "pay ya back tomorra" took place at my end of the table. I hated it when the hot lunch program came into being during my high school years. The food put out by the cooks couldn't compare with Mama's brown bag lunches, and the first meal I ate in the cafeteria was an unforgettable experience, etched for time and eternity into my brain!

The younger kids had gotten rid of all the food before we high school students, who were housed in another building, could walk up the hill for our meal. The cooks, staring in utter desperation at the long line of semi-starved teen-agers waiting to be served, started frantically chopping wieners into tiny bits and opening enormous cans of beans. Such was my introduction to "The Nutritious Hot Lunch Program." That meal never even got close to a stove. Kids of today would destroy the building if food like that was placed on their trays.

By far the most unusual area of the basement had to be the furnace room, where our janitor held forth and ruled with an iron fist. His big room looked a lot like my idea of Hell, with the flames licking out through air slots in the heavy iron door, while steam hissed and escaped through vents and cracks. Uncle Wooly-Worm (I don't know why we called him that, but we all did), sat in one corner going through the tossed away lunch sacks to salvage any remaining scraps of food to take home for hog feed. (Is it true that today any leftovers from the school lunch program must be put down the garbage disposal? Uncle Wooly-Worm would turn over in his grave!)

The first floor contained classrooms where the quest for knowledge began. In those days before the advent of kindergarten, our introduction to education took place in FIRST GRADE, always seen in capital letters in the mind's eye of a small child.

Woe unto the hapless little ones who ran into a bad teacher at the start of his learning experience. I'm happy to report my first grade teacher, Miss Lenore, was wonderful. She was pretty, easy to get along with, and smelled good! What more could be asked for in a teacher? I loved her so much that at the end of school I couldn't control my tears and cried so hard I was embarrassed to line up with the other kids for a good-bye hug. I ran home, grabbed two chocolate cupcakes which were cooling on the kitchen table, and went to bed to console myself with food. (Having followed this practice religiously through my life, I can highly recommend it as withstanding the test of time far better than tranquilizers. It's cheaper and a lot more pleasant!)

The second, third and fourth grade classrooms were also located on the first floor, as well as a small library which we were permitted to utilize when our assigned work was completed.

The second floor was home to the rest of the school and included (God help us all!) Miss Williams, our fifth grade teacher and the meanest human being ever to embrace professional education. We loved to hate this loathsome creature, scathingly referred to by those of us who were well-read as "Attila the Hun."

In those days teachers were permitted to chastise students in just about any way they saw fit, short of capital punishment, and some of us weren't absolutely sure Miss Williams had not received special dispensation from the Pope to invoke the death penalty. Her favorite means of torture was pulling hair, and it didn't take any great offense to set her off. Most of our class had endured a creative rearrangement of our mane due to her ill temper and it hurt. Believe me, it hurt!

My boyfriend, Jacob, whom I loved dearly, hated her even more passionately than the rest of the group. He had a head full of lovely blond curls which almost daily caught the attention of "Attila." (Jacob was not by any stretch of the imagination a good child. The religious fanaticism which had caused his mother to name her children from the Bible had in no way rubbed off on him. The beautiful little boy was meaner than a junkyard dog, and we all followed him slavishly down the path of wickedness.)

One day toward the end of school Jacob (who in all probability had prayed a good deal about it and possibly received inspiration from above), developed a wonderfully diabolical scheme which he felt in all probability would result in the death of Miss Williams. If it didn't kill her, he thought, it would surely cause a complete and total mental collapse, and she would be taken to the asylum for what remained of her life. We could live with that. In those days nervous breakdowns were not at all uncommon in the field of education. (As a matter of fact, they are not uncommon in the field of education even today.)

Now Jacob's plan hinged greatly on the fact that Miss Williams had bargained with one of her students to bring a pint of milk with which she augmented her sack lunch each day. The school lunch program had not as yet reared its ugly head and this practice of teachers buying raw milk was fairly common. (Mama kept a cow in the back yard, as did many townsfolk, but I would have died and rotted before giving this evil teacher any sort of sustenance. She paid a nickel a day for the milk, no small sum back then, but I had my pride!)

One day at recess Jacob filled us in on his plan. "Y'all lissen to me now an' I'll tell ya what I'm fixin' to do. Brang me some fishin' worms, and roly-poly bugs..." and as our young leader enlightened us, we became amazed at his idea.

It was beautiful...utterly, completely, beautiful...simplicity itself. And in our hearts we knew it would not fail.

Each day, right before lunch (until the hoped-for collapse occurred and our purveyor of education was reduced to either gibbering idiocy or death), Jacob planned to drop into her milk objects of an extremely foreign nature. Sickening stuff. Like rat droppings. The entire class was sworn to secrecy and THE TREATMENT, as we voted to call our project, was to go into effect on April 1st.

On day ONE of THE TREATMENT, Jacob surreptitiously dropped a small rock into the milk, which caused Miss Williams to choke and sputter a bit, but she got it down and couldn't prove a thing. The milk deliverer was

21

told to report the incident to his parents, who would surely be more careful in the future.

Day TWO was a little worse. A small worm and two roly-poly bugs were put in the jar and when Miss Williams saw them bobbing about in her drink, the results were predictable. While she was attacking our heads, Jacob removed the offending objects, and she again was left without proof of a problem.

Day THREE saw the culmination of THE TREAT-MENT. God forgive me, but it was wonderful! When she removed the lid from her Mason jar and spied a very small mouse frantically attempting to remove itself from the milky bath, that was it! As we say in the hills, "She broke and run!" for the office of the principal and fell into his arms, babbling incoherently.

We liked the new teacher well enough except that she kept insisting we write little notes to Miss Williams. We were allowed to quit when the asylum sent word that our former teacher did not seem to enjoy our correspondence and was causing a big mess when she ripped the letters into tiny pieces.

You can imagine what a thrill we got from hearing that report.

Chapter 5

ATHENS BY THE RAILROAD TRACK

To be perfectly truthful, not a soul in town could say that an intensive search for culture was all that high on the list of priorities in our community. We were pretty far back in the hills and our refinements were few, but we liked it like that. We made do with what we had.

The railroad running through town proved advantageous to those of us who yearned for foreign travel. We could satisfy our wanderlust by meeting one or both of the passenger trains which rolled through each day and paused briefly to discharge and pick up the folks lucky enough to afford the fare. If time permitted (and we usually had time to spare), we would go and wave to the traveling public, wondering where they were from and to what strange, exotic places they might be going; Hardy, Jonesboro, maybe even that great metropolitan center of the South, Memphis! (Dear Lord, how I wanted to go to Memphis, and I got to when I was about seven. My kind Aunt Flo helped me make the trip.)

23

A shady, well-kept lawn surrounded the old railroad station and was the favored place for a somewhat unusual event which occurred each day...the influx of unemployed, laid-off, and "extra board" workers who played checkers with one another while waiting for a job to materialize.

All these men, young and old, sat and spat and watched the girls of the town do what little shopping they could afford. The town idlers passed many a lurid and lascivious comment concerning the physical attributes of the more curvaceous beauties as they jiggled past.

"Goin' ta play checkers" was the excuse given the wives of all these loafers when they left home each morning, but I had it on good authority that most of them were just waiting for the daily arrival of the local beauty queen, Bobbie Jo Bilderback. The sensual Bobbie Jo was about seventeen, blond, and in the vernacular of the hills, "built like a brick outhouse!" The resemblance never came totally clear to me, but I was not one to argue overlong with local opinion.

In the thirties, any girl even pretending to be "decent" did not appear in town wearing shorts, but Bobbie Jo's body wrapped in a tight skirt and even tighter sweater left little to the imagination of the sweating male population. (Several mothers of teenage boys had their preacher get up a petition requesting that Bobbie Jo's parents lock her up in the smokehouse until she either got married or reached fifty, whichever came first. The Bilderbacks took umbrage and left the church.)

I wonder whatever happened to her. Maybe when the men went back to work and the checker games declined, she started staying home to help her mother. Naw...

Our town claimed the only "opry house" in southern Missouri, and this beautiful brick edifice was host to numerous theatrical productions early in the century. By the time I came along, it was serving mostly as City Hall, and housed the local public library, which was my home away from home. (Alas, a subtraction was done about thirty years ago which removed the top floor and what I always thought of as "the tower room," and now this landmark of my early years serves as the town jail. You wanna talk about progress...?)

When I was six or seven years old an intellectual fad of sorts seized the town. Small children were trained by one of the local teachers who had majored in drama to memorize poetry and prose, complete with gesticulations varied and colorful, for the entertainment and edification of friends, family, church, school, and the community in general.

This cultural phenomenon was termed, if memory serves me, "expressional training," and without fear of contradiction by any who witnessed my act, I can say that I was good at it!

Yes, at the risk of sounding conceited, I must tell you I had little or no competition in the field. Few gatherings or entertainments were considered complete until I had said my "piece," and people would stop on the street corner to point me out as "that kid that it don't bother a bit to git up in front of a crowd a people an' talk fer an hour an' a half."

As a general rule, when our group was preparing to stage a glorious production of rhetorical eloquence, the teacher would assign us each a poem or story to recite. But if given a choice, I always elected to deliver a work of art called "The Crooked Mouth Family." Gladly would I spew forth this literary masterpiece, complete with twisted mouth, excruciatingly horrible nasal tones, and a resonance which would have made George Bernard Shaw lie down and die. Truly, I gave a spectacular performance.

Lots of days as I walked home from school, elderly ladies would call me into their homes for a spur of the moment private "recitation," and I was always happy to comply. They usually rewarded me with food and drink, plus praising my talents to the sky, and I have ever had a weakness for all of the above. You must remember, too, in those days parents didn't have to worry about their offspring being abducted, maltreated, and dismembered by crazed killers. Mama never worried about me so long as I showed up at home by suppertime.

One memorable afternoon I was called into the residence of a lovely, cultured lady who had been one of Daddy's teachers. He loved Miss Jessie dearly, as indeed did most of the town, and I certainly wanted to put on a good show for her. She would, without a doubt, make it a point to report on me to Daddy, telling him what a great gift he had given to the world in the form of his talented daughter, Martha, and he liked to hear that. (Such favorable reports on his children were rare. Practically nonexistent).

Miss Jessie had the advantage, unknown to most small town families, of INSIDE PLUMBING, and I determined to avail myself of the opportunity to explore such unknown luxury.

This sweet and gracious lady was pleased to answer in the affirmative when I requested the use of her bathroom. (Little did she know what I had in mind!) After a considerable length of time elapsed, she came in to check on me. Perhaps she thought, rightly, that I was not familiar with the intricate workings of her commode.

What a sight met her eyes! My clothes were scattered all over the floor and I was up to my ears in hot water, bath salts, and perfumed bubbles. To this day I can remember luxuriating in the huge, porcelain, claw-footed monster of a bathing vessel, so far removed from the metal laundry tub of my Saturday night experiences.

Dear Miss Jessie laughed till she cried, then dried me off and laughed a lot more when I gave my rendition of "The Crooked Mouth Family."

I was never better!

Chapter 6

DADDY TAKES ON A BIG BUSINESS

When we were little, children used to go around the neighborhood door to door and sell stuff to those folks whose sales resistance was weak. Hot items being pushed were garden seeds, assorted greeting cards (usually of a highly religious nature), and cardboard wall plaques which beseeched the Almighty to "BLESS THIS HOUSE." (The lettering was in silver glitter, and against a garish red background the communication really stood out. Mama Cash had invested in one of the little placards and placed it near the head of her bed. Since the message glowed in the dark for a long time after the light was out, the words were quite reassuring to me when I spent the night with her and slept at the foot of the bed. With God and Mama Cash both on watch, I was sure nothing could get me.)

Another big product touted by these youthful entrepreneurs were flowers made out of crepe paper. Almost obscenely colorful, the blossoms were usually produced by the seller's grandmother. Sometimes they were put into large glass fruit jars and placed on the graves of departed loved ones, there to fade away in the summer sun and winter rain until only a pale memory remained. (To this very day I don't like fake flowers. Perhaps they are a sad reminder to me of the difficult financial circumstances which forced so many families to such a pitiful floral tribute.)

Money was scarce as hen's teeth in the thirties, so most folks couldn't buy anything no matter how touching the young salesperson's presentation. But occasionally one of the kids would make a sale and earn one of the highly praised prizes offered by the home office. Heading the list of rewards for excellence in selling would be Red Ryder gloves, sling-shots, or possibly a year's subscription to a magazine of your choice. (I was always partial to *Grit*.)

Though we desperately wanted to earn spending money, our clan was not permitted to take part in wealth-making projects of this nature. Daddy held the strong opinion that such enterprises took unfair advantage of friends and neighbors, and as a rule the little salespeople didn't come by our house but once in their careers. (Daddy died at an early age and didn't get in on the "home sales party." I try not to think what he would have to say on that subject.)

Since there was no way we could have been on any mailing lists, it was a mystery to the whole family how the Red Hollyhock Salve sales force happened on the name of my young brother, Reg. But he received through the mail, clearly marked with his full name, a complete retailing kit consisting of several gross of the aforementioned medical product. (He was all of six years old at the time and you want to talk about inexperienced in salesmanship? Reg couldn't talk plain until he was in the third grade, and being of a shy and retiring nature anyway, he avoided contact with the outside world if at all possible. A more unlikely candidate to go out and peddle salve could not have been found had the whole county been searched.)

Included in the total package was a colorful brochure, vividly describing the many youths living in the hill country, as was Reg, who were becoming ridiculously wealthy in their spare time. To further whet his appetite for greater things to come, they enclosed a free gift, euphemistically called a "singing lariat." This little toy amounted to a narrow piece of crepe paper on a short string which when whirled about the head resulted in a colorful circle. If you possessed a lively imagination, you just might possibly hear a humming noise, though none of us ever could. (You can guess about how long a plaything of this fragility lasted in our rambunctious household.)

Feeling as strongly as he did about kiddy salesmen, Daddy certainly had no intention of permitting my little brother to make a fool of himself in the community by conducting a neighborhood canvas concerning the medical needs of individual households. The hundreds of cans of salve were shoved under the bed and unless we needed some for a chigger or tick bite or as a lubrication for sidewalk roller skates, the incident was forgotten.

Then the letters started.

About a month had gone by when Reg received a nice, friendly letter from the staff of Red Hollyhock inquiring as to his success with their product. They casually mentioned a young lad in a joining county who had just finished building his family a small mansion with savings from a three year partnership with Red Hollyhock, and they wanted to encourage Reg to scour the town for his part of the easy money to be had.

Daddy did not dignify it with a reply. He just frowned a bit as he threw it in the fire.

In a few more weeks another letter came, not so

pleasant this time and mentioning that the company had not heard a word from Reg. It stressed highly the need of pushing for sales and reminded my brother of the riches in which he might be wallowing with just a bit of after school and weekend endeavor. This one was ignored, too, though Daddy fumed and cussed a bit.

Nothing really exciting happened until the third and final letter was received in which Red Hollyhock revealed its intentions of starting legal proceedings against Reg. (Remember, we are talking here about a six year old child.)

Lest I offend someone, I will leave to the reader's imagination the great and colorful conversation which took place following the reading of the final letter. Suffice it to say that the Great God Almighty was addressed in rhetorical eloquence never since equaled by Daddy.

Then, aided by advice which we could but assume came from on high, he composed a letter forceful in the extreme!

The entire firm of Red Hollyhock Salve Company, plus all the stockholders, was included in the fiery epistle which began by stating that the !@#$% salve had not been requested by any one in the Cash family. It went on to inform the company that the product certainly wasn't wanted, and in closing remarks the information was passed on to the shipping department that the only way they would get their !@#$% salve back was to come after it! (I am leaving out a lot of the good part.)

Red Hollyhock Salve Company seemed to lose all interest in Reg after they received the letter, and our family was left with a more than lifetime supply of the miracle drug of the thirties. We were generous in sharing with the whole county.

Farm boys used a lot of it on little pigs following a rather crude type of surgery, but even so it was around for a long time.

Chapter 7

BROTHER, COULD HE SPARE A DIME!

During my growing up years small children would do almost anything for a dime. You could buy a lot with this tiny coin. Double-dip ice cream cones were to be had for a nickel, and you could see a Saturday afternoon double-feature at Peck's Theater for just ten cents. Best of all, a dime properly invested in jelly beans or B.B.Bat suckers at Le Fleur's School Store would purchase a whole day of popularity. (Remember B.B.Bat suckers? They were available in strawberry, chocolate, or banana, and guaranteed to last eight hours or until a tooth broke, whichever came first.)

Our parents could not give us money very often. Two cents on the Lord's Day for Sunday School offering was about it. (Some of the kids held back a penny when the collection plate came around, but I was always afraid to for fear God would get me!)

But I did want money. It seemed the very lack of it spurred me on, and I was led into many and varied schemes. Drawn by an overwhelming lust for wealth, my entrepreneurship knew no bounds.

I have sold blackberries for ten cents a gallon. Picking them was an excruciating ordeal for me because of my life-long allergy to chiggers, and it seemed the evil red mites were aware of my problem. The suffering which came about after a trip to the berry patch was simply endured, for in those days kids weren't taken to the doctor for allergy shots. Most of us had sense enough to scratch.

Baby-sitting the neighbor's kids all day plus doing some ironing while the little ones napped would also bring in a dime. We were fortunate enough to live within walking distance of a fairly wealthy family, and I picked up several small jobs from them.

I remember at one point in my young life selling raw milk around town. Carrying such heavy glass bottles up and down the many hills in an awkward wire container had to be good for my waistline, but before I could achieve much in the way of a figure we were shut down by the health department. The town suffered an outbreak of salmonella food poisoning (for which we were erroneously blamed), so rather than face a lawsuit we closed out the dairy business.

Probably the most gut wrenching and terrifying fund-raising opportunity I ever embraced took place within the bosom of my own family. It had to do with a unique little game which we referred to by the lengthy but completely self-explanatory title of "Getting Locked Up in the Icebox While Daddy Counts to Fifty and Then He'll Give You a Dime!"

Now this game was originated, so far as any family member knows, by Daddy, who had what some might call a rather warped sense of humor. He and Mama had to struggle to make a living for their large family, but Daddy

34

was a fun-loving person and usually had some action
going which included us kids.

Of course the game centered around an old, wooden
icebox which normally held a large chunk of ice. The ap-
pliance was somewhat automatic in that if Mama forgot to
dump the drain pan before she went to bed, she
automatically got to mop up the melted water the next
morning. The overflow from the melted ice served to keep
the kitchen floor clean, but it did nothing to help Mama's
disposition. (Those of you over fifty probably know exactly what I am describing.)

Usually about twice a summer, on a Sunday afternoon
when all the food had gone bad because we had run out of
ice, Mama would, to quote her, "take the icebox to a good
cleaning." She would scrub out the inside with baking
soda (considered by most housewives to be the deodorant
and disinfectant wonder of the Depression years), take out
all the dividers and leave the doors open to (another quote)
"let it air out."

Sometime during the course of the afternoon Daddy
would casually remark (and we all knew by the look on his
face what was coming), "Who around here is brave
enough to let me shut 'em up in the icebox? I'll count to
fifty and then let ya out. Give ya a dime..."

Always the fool and poor to the point of desperation, I
raced to head the line. The icebox was not greatly com-
modious, and it was necessary to back into the compart-
ment, a task not easy for me. Being a rather corpulent,
short, and stockily-built child, I had to squeeze, fold, and
grunt a lot, but I always got in there! Often Clark would
shove me in the face extremely hard and that helped.

Then came the horrible, heart-stopping moment when
the door would slowly close. (I don't know why, but Daddy always closed it slowly.)

35

Now like you, I have never been buried alive, so it is impossible for me to say with absolute certainty that this experience equaled premature interment, but I'd like to bet my bottom dollar that it would run a pretty close second. The icebox was white enamel on the inside, and when the door finally shut, ever so slowly, sometimes mashing my nose (depending on how my head was situated), it just had to be comparable to a coffin lid making its last closure.

Finally, I would hear Daddy say, "O.K. Martha. Now I'll count to fifty and then I'll let ya out."

Having played this game before, I knew as well as I knew my own name that he was not going to let me out when he got to fifty. Never in all the times I had volunteered to be incarcerated had he ever released me just when the count was finished. Yet the optimist in me kept saying, "Maybe, just maybe, this time is going to be different," while the pessimist countered with, "You gotta be kiddin'!"

Daddy would count rather loud and fairly fast until he got to about forty. Then he would slow down. The counting practically ceased.

Eventually, when he finally reached the magic number, I'd sing out, ever hopeful that he would be merciful and release me, "O.K. Daddy, lemme out fast 'cause I'm runnin' outta air and can't breathe good!"

Now right here is where the fun began for the group waiting outside. They all had a pretty good idea, as I did, just what Daddy was going to reply to my plea for release.

"O.K. sweetheart, but I believe I'll get me a drink first."

At this point my nerves, already stretched right up to the breaking point, would give way like a rotten rubber band and from somewhere way down deep, I obtained enough air to begin my wild, piercing howls for emancipation.

I knew when I had screamed for a bit he would let me out. That was part of the game. But I always feared that one day something might "get" Daddy and I would be left holed up until the ice man delivered on Monday. Mama and the other kids possibly would save me, but gut level I knew they didn't actually like me very much because I was fat, and they very probably would seize upon this opportunity to get rid of a family embarrassment.

He always seemed to know just how much I could stand, and right before I died Daddy would let me out of my place of captive employment, give me a dime and laugh until he cried. By this time the audience usually held several of the Jones kids who had been drawn to our home by the intensity of my screams.

The same job opportunity was offered to them, but they always declined, saying it was almost suppertime and they needed to get on home.

37

Chapter 8

TOWN CHARACTERS

Most small towns come equipped with a few citizens who add quite a lot of color to the local scene, and in our little village we had our share. Believe me, we had our share.

One elderly gentlemen was totally deaf. He couldn't hear a gun if it was shot off right behind his back. (I know because I saw some of the kids try it one day). He spent his days walking around the streets with his head down. Way down. Sunk right down on his chest. For years I thought he was extremely sad, but I finally figured out what he was doing. (Even in early childhood I was not really bright.) He made his living looking for stuff, mostly money, but he'd pick up anything of value he came across. Then he would sell it to someone for a fraction of its original cost. Occasionally he'd bring something into our little grocery store and Daddy would buy it (if he could at all justify the purchase), because he thought the old man was nice. Just a bit different. Actually, a lot different.

Another resident walked. He walked almost ceaselessly, and he walked fast! In an age when most transportation needs were met with one's own two feet, this fellow had walking down to a fine art. He always refused a ride when offered, saying, "No, thanks, I'm in a hurry." Now it's true that cars didn't go very fast back then, but still you'd think when it was raining... He'd fit right in with the walking craze of today.

The shops in town served as gathering places for these characters, and Daddy's store was no exception. The men would come in around lunchtime to eat some cheese and crackers, and they would stay on to swap licentious gossip about the local beauty queen, Bobbie Jo Bilderback.

One of the regulars had an extremely loud voice and, like so many fellows of the time, consumed a good bit of the local liquor which did absolutely nothing to decrease his conversational tone.

One afternoon Mama sent me downtown for a pound of coffee, and I walked in the store just in time to hear Pete roar, "SEE THAT S.O.B. ACROSS THE STREET? I AIN'T GOT NO USE FOR HIM A'TALL. HE DRANKS TOO MUCH, HE CUSSES REAL BAD, AND BESIDES THAT, HE TALKS WAY TOO LOUD." There is an old hill expression which says, "It takes one to know one."

But without doubt, all these characters paled into oblivion when compared with our neighbor, Miss Pearlie Maxine Devereau. This maiden lady of indeterminate origin and age was looked upon with deep suspicion by most of the adults in the community because, unlike most other hill people, Miss Pearlie Maxine did not hold the truth in high regard.

Mama often said, "That woman would climb a tree to lie when she could sit in her rockin' chair on the front porch and tell the truth." (Mama tried to guide us in the

40

right way with moral sayings of that nature but we ignored her. We all felt Miss Pearlie Maxine to be the most fascinating woman of the age, way out in front of Mama.) Needless to say, Mama was one of the folks who looked upon our unusual friend with much skepticism.

In spite of the fact that this teller-of-falsehoods looked a great deal like the witch in "Hansel and Gretel," we kids worshiped the ground she walked on. She maintained a large menagerie of animals, both tame and wild, and we were permitted to play with them all as long as no harm came to child or beast. Futhermore, she was an excellent cook and seemed to delight in furnishing her admirers with cakes, pies, and cookies of a most delicious nature. Never once did she say, "You'd better not eat so much. You'll spoil your supper." Experience had taught her that our stomachs had a lot in common with bottomless pits.

But the attraction which drew us to Miss Pearlie Maxine, as metal is drawn to a magnet, had to be her complete and total disregard for anything even remotely resembling reality. She truly seemed to believe the outlandish stories with which she mesmerized us.

One day when I inquired why she had her arm in a sling, she answered, "I was on the back porch a couple of nights ago, gettin' some sweet potatoes fer supper, and there was this great big coon sorta hunkered down under my bench. Now I jest know he was fixin' to carry off my potatoes, 'cause when I took after that rascal with my broom, he jumped on my back and knocked me plumb off the porch. My arm's nearly broke!"

She did have a high back porch, so I guess her story could have been true. Sympathy for her plight just oozed out of me while I enjoyed some fresh gingerbread still warm from the oven.

Miss Pearlie Maxine's home was just down the hill from

our place, and we visited her often. One afternoon as I neared the house I spied a small goat in her calf pen. This really excited me for it hadn't been too long since our pet goat, Billy Waddles, almost a family member, had hanged himself, and I selfishly thought the goat might possibly be a replacement for our lost pet.

"Where'd ya git him?" I anxiously questioned my friend, as she invited me in for cookies. She got herself a cup of coffee, handed me a dozen gingersnaps, looked me right in the eye, and began her explanation. It was good. Even for her, it was good.

"Martha," she started, "I was layin' in bed last night... musta been sometime around midnight...when I heard a loud thump on the roof, and I jumped outta bed and ran to the back yard. There was that little ol' goat just bleatin' and kickin' like it was fixin' to die. It come to me to throw it in the rain barrel, and I guess that saved its life, 'cause it seems fine this mornin'." And then she added the clincher. "Only thing I can figger is it fell out of an airplane."

Miss Pearlie Maxine had grown up in northern Arkansas, not far from our community, and we often heard amazing tales of happenings that took place in that region during her childhood. One of my favorite stories concerned the razorback hogs which prowled the Arkansas mountains. She offered the following tale as proof positive that the Arkansas razorback, at least in the days of her youth, was well-nigh indestructible.

"My daddy," her testimony began, "was diggin' up stumps in some new ground one day, just about to kill hisself tryin' to pry 'em up with a pick-ax, when one of them county agents come around to visit. While they was talkin' the agent told Daddy about a new way to get rid of stumps... with dynamite!"

Her daddy, she continued, was pleased as punch to find

an alternative method of getting the infernal stumps out of the ground, and immediately he hitched the team and drove to the store to get the dynamite, fuse, and caps.

When he got back home, he very carefully followed to the letter the instructions of the county agent. He set the charge, lighted the fuse, and ran for cover. But for some reason the fuse went out and since it was getting dark, he decided to wait until morning before trying again.

Early next morning a big, old razorback hog found the stick of dynamite and, curiosity getting the better of him, he ate the whole thing. Being a hog, and still hungry, he went down to the barn where he attempted to steal some corn from the mule, who quite naturally tried to kick him. For the first and last time in its life, the mule connected with its target, and the dynamite went off.

"Gosh," we all groaned in sympathy. "That must have been an awful mess."

"Yeah," Miss Pearlie Maxine agreed. "Yeah, it really wuz. Killed the mule, wrecked the barn, broke ever winda in the house, and for nearly a week we had an awful sick hog!"

We began to appreciate the antics of our odd little neighbor even more during the terrible years of World War II. As in the rest of the world, life grew pretty harsh in the hills. She brought some measure of humor to our rather drab existence.

We were enduring the absence of family members off fighting God only knew where, battling ration coupons, and listening to grim daily news reports on the radio. We were hearing with dismay the locally held suspicion that our neighbors, a German family, were up to their ears in espionage. (It was amazing to me that Hitler's headquarters might have been interested in anything that happened in Oregon County. We were about as far removed from civilization and any organized war effort as a group of people could possibly be.)

Early in the thirties, Miss Pearlie Maxine had fallen deeply in love with President Roosevelt, and she let out the word of a torrid correspondence going on between Fair, Missouri and Washington, D.C. with herself and FDR as the principals involved. (Miss Pearlie Maxine shared the opinion of most of the folks in our part of the world who considered our national leader to be the "Savior of the Working Man.")

Oddly enough, she never allowed anyone to see her replies from this long distance lover, but she was happy to answer any questions put to her about his handling of world affairs. After the Oak Ridge secret became public knowledge, she confessed to having been privy to the information for years. Only a few folks believed her. I was one of them.

You can imagine what a severe emotional blow was hers when word was received of the untimely death of our president. In those days older hill ladies sometimes "went into mourning" and Miss Pearlie Maxine was not seen on the street without her black veil for a long time.

The neighborhood kids helped her organize and conduct a very impressive memorial service each year on the anniversary of President Roosevelt's passing. We usually held it in the goat pen, and most of the time the Jones girls sang "Precious Memories."

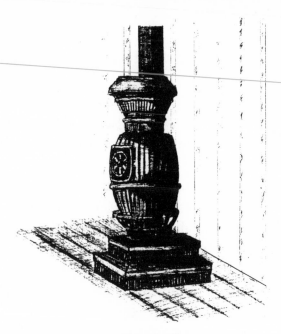

Chapter 9

LIFE IN A HOME FREEZER

Winter was not my favorite season as a child. I can't remember anything pleasant about cold weather except Christmas, and the holiday didn't last long enough to out-weigh carrying in all that wood for five months.

Even all my Christmas memories aren't monumentally great. One year I got a toy piano, which just tickled me to death, and Clark got a tool box, complete with a small hammer. He, a curious-minded child, questioned how the piano could produce noise and quickly started an in-depth investigation with the hammer as his principal tool of research. End of piano!

Before central heating reached Oregon County, the population got chilly sometime in October and didn't really warm up until the following May. Our winter won-derland seemed to last an intolerably long time.

During cold weather, most bedrooms were shut off from the supply of heat, which in the majority of homes was a wood-burning stove. Those bedrooms got COLD, believe me, and crossing the linoleum covered floor bare-footed was a horrendous ordeal. (House shoes were an unknown luxury in our family.) Somewhere in the far northern extremities of the world's arctic region there may possibly be some substance colder than a floor covered with linoleum but as yet I have not found it.

Our survival lay in running as fast as possible from the comparative warmth of the living room to the questionable haven of the bed. We almost froze before we could crawl into our dubious refuge, so heavy with quilts that a small child was hard put to turn over without help.

Daddy would not permit us to keep a fire burning all night since the danger of a house fire was so great. He didn't have a lot of confidence in Mama's ability to react rationally under stress, and I've heard him say many times if the house ever caught on fire while he was gone (which was a lot of the time) he knew without a shadow of a doubt that Clair and the kids would burn up before the neighbors could save them. Daddy was not by any stretch of the imagination an unduly optimistic person, but we never had a house fire, and many of our friends did.

Since we were not permitted to keep a fire going during the night, we devised another use for the stove, and if I do say so myself, it was clever! Shortly before bedtime we dismantled the stove, carefully removing all the parts not securely fastened with bolts. Then we meticulously wrapped the various segments with towels, and took them to bed with us in lieu of hot-water bottles or heating pads. (I always tried to be first to retire so I could grab one of the large footrests to cuddle close to my numbed body after the horribly frigid trip to bed.)

It helped a lot. The metal from the stove retained some semblance of warmth for five or six minutes, after which it was shoved to a far corner of the bed. Touching the stove part accidentally after it cooled was equivalent to receiving an electric shock treatment and an experience not greatly to be desired!

One year our family wintered in town due to the anticipated birth of Reg, the only non-September baby in our clan. The big, old rented house was little more than a barn, totally lacking insulation, central heating, underpinning, or any of the other niceties of civilization we now deem necessities.

But to us kids it seemed absolutely luxurious, because the cold water faucet found in the kitchen meant we didn't have to pump or draw water from a well or cistern and carry it into the house. (Drawing water on a bitter, winter morning is not one of the greatest pleasures life has to offer. Trust me on this one!)

Also in the kitchen (though certainly not as modern as the cold water tap) was a wood-burning cookstove. With the help of this monstrosity Mama cooked the greatest food imaginable. With the cookstove going full blast it was reasonably warm in the kitchen, which was nice because we also used one corner as our dining area. But after supper was over, the fire in the stove was allowed to go out and the kitchen door was shut, closing the room off from any source of heat. It got cold in there!

This was a two story house, and shortly before bedtime we opened the door which led upstairs to our sleeping area. Our science teacher had told us that heat rises, and we held out hope that warmth from the living room stove would drift up to temper the polar regions above. (It never got warm upstairs until sometime in June when it became unbearably hot, again making sleep unusual.)

One bitterly cold evening not long before bedtime, we heard a loud noise from the kitchen, but loud noises were fairly common in a household such as ours. None of us

47

rushed to investigate since Bert, climbing to search for hidden cookies, had turned the kitchen cabinet over on himself several times in the past. (He was never badly hurt from such mishaps, but the glass front on the cabinet was demolished by the first upset. Mama had to string a little flour sack curtain over the empty space to keep the flies off her dishes. In those days, women had to be innovative because there was no money to replace the broken glass in a cabinet door.)

As I said, we just thought Bert was at it again, but we were wrong. Yes, we were terribly wrong, and unfortunately Daddy was the first to realize just how wrong we were. When he went into the kitchen for a pre-bed drink of water we heard his body hit the floor with considerable force, and the intensity of his screams caused us to run quickly to his aid.

Well, a nightmare scene met our eyes! Water was spraying wildly from the single tap which had frozen, ruptured, and pulled away from the wall, causing the loud noise we heard earlier. Daddy was sprawled on the floor, having taken quite a fall due to the thin layer of ice which had frozen on the kitchen linoleum due to the unintentional shower. (Remember, we are talking about COLD floors.)

He was not suffering in silence. "My arm! My arm!" he screamed in a manner which bespoke considerable pain. "Great God Almighty! I've broken my arm!" We had a pretty good idea that the arm in question was not broken, since he was waving it wildly in Mama's face while continuing his heavenly conversation.

Mama burst into tears and tried to help him rise from the floor. Being in an advanced state of pregnancy, she could not accomplish a whole lot. (Looking back from a mature viewpoint, I can see it is a thousand wonders she didn't fall and bring about the premature birth of Reg, but luck was with us. Loosely speaking.)

Eventually we got the neighbors to come in and help us get Daddy to his feet. They did not seem to relish the task for Daddy was not a great one to cooperate while in a state of excruciating agony.

When the situation stabilized somewhat, we kids crept silently up the stairs, not daring even to giggle until we were safely covered under the mounds of quilts which kept us alive during the cold winter nights.

Then there was another explosion of noise, but of a completely different nature. Laughter!

Chapter 10

THE RACE IS ON

"The night that thang nearly got ole Reg" was a topic of conversation for a long time around our house. Everyone in the neighborhood heard about it, and I'm willing to bet my bottom dollar there are folks in the Oregon County region even unto this very day who could relate the episode as easily as I can.

My little brothers, Bert and Reg, loved to hunt, and our place was almost surrounded by woods which continued for miles past the back fields. They could walk for hours in the hills, perfecting their skills in marksmanship while providing much needed meat for the table. The boys had only one gun and since they liked to hunt together, taking turns using the weapon, Daddy was concerned for their safety. He came up with a pretty good plan; one of them would carry the gun and the other would have control of the shells. If they got into a wild argument while on the hunt, killing each other would not be easy.

Since Mama had never heard of child molesters, serial

51

killers, drug addicts and many of the other niceties of our present day society, she never worried about any of us so long as we made it home by suppertime. Even then she didn't seem to worry a lot. (There were eight of us kids in the grand total, and when I was rearing my own child I grew to understand her seeming lack of concern. One can only worry so much; then one grows numb. Mama had been numb for years.)

On the evening of "the night..." we were lined up on benches around the table, all in our respective places with the exception of Reggie. His absence was not noticed for a while since one of the neighbor kids had slipped into his place, a not unusual occurrence. (We all played widely around the area and frequently ate at a friend's house if sundown caught up with us and we couldn't make it home for the evening meal. Total food consumption and time spent in preparation per child pretty well evened out over a year's time because Mama fed other people's children about as often as they fed hers. No big issue was ever made so long as the extra child was well-behaved and relatively quiet.)

It's possible we wouldn't have noticed the switch in kids at all if Mama hadn't mentioned, between her many trips to the stove for more biscuits, that the faint screams coming from the woods sounded a lot like Reg. We all stopped eating long enough to agree with her, and at this point the neighbor child's presence was commented upon and Reggie's absence noted.

Perhaps this would be the appropriate time to mention that Reg was the different one in the family. Mama thought it was probably because he had been born in February, whereas the rest of us had birthdays in September. Reg was quiet, fair, rather mannerly, and large for his years as opposed to the rest of us who were noisy, dark as

52

Indians, and as rude as we thought prudent.

(Incidentally, I can recall Daddy saying, in later years when mention was made of our glut of September birthdays, that he knew exactly what triggered the demise of the large family in the United States of America. He vowed it was the advent of central heating and electric blankets, and not the wide-spread use of birth control measures, as some believed. He could have been right. We did not argue much with Daddy.)

When the realization hit him that Reg was not with us, Daddy reacted in his usual way.

"Where in the name of the Great God Almighty is that boy?" he screamed. Unlike Mama, he seemed to worry about us a lot and frequently enlisted the aid of the Deity in caring for the family. "Don't I have enough to worry about," he further questioned his creator in a quivering shriek, "without these kids disappearing at mealtime? God help me, where could he be?!"

(Our father's tendency to become highly emotional could be quite unnerving to first time visitors, but through the years the family had grown accustomed to his rantings. We never so much as missed a bite.)

The cries from the woods were rapidly becoming louder, and we all agreed it must be ole Reg all right, though none of us could say we had ever previously heard the young boy make such an effort to express himself. Bert said he guessed he'd better see what was going on, and after admonishing the entire table to leave his food alone, he grabbed the old lantern hanging on a nail by the back door and quickly left.

As Bert approached the barn (he later told us), the wild, maniacal cries continued to grow in intensity, and he broke into a trot, which promptly became a run. Fearful that Reggie would lose all control and possibly have a stroke or a massive heart attack before help reached him, Bert gave it all he had.

Rounding the last of the old outbuildings, he could see little Reg emerging from the edge of the woods, arms fully extended and flailing wildly while with each step he uttered the wild, piercing scream which had originally caught our attention.

Bert called out to Reg, hoping to assure him that help was near, but to no avail. Nothing could get through to the terrified child, whose only thought was to reach safety at home in the bosom of his family. As a final resort, Bert attempted (rather foolishly, as it turned out), to step directly into the path of the desperate lad, thinking his brother would see him and stop. Such was not the case! Reg quite simply knocked Bert flat, stepped on his face several times, and continued his hysterical flight to home and the security of his kin.

(Bert remarked later that he would have been a lot more likely to stop a runaway freight train than to stop Reg that evening.)

Meanwhile, we at the supper table were waiting in stunned silence. Even Daddy was momentarily quiet. We had not long to wait. The screen door suddenly and completely disintegrated as Reg fell through, prone, prostrate, and stretched full length on the kitchen floor. He kicked weakly once, and then all movement ceased, save for the slight flow of blood from deep scratches about his head and face.

Everyone thought he was dead, I'm sure, though none of us gave voice to that sad opinion. We all reacted in different ways to the disaster. Mama immediately burst into tears, which was nothing new. My older sister, Anne, who considered herself somewhat of an authority on first aid by reason of a Girl Scout badge, ran for a dipper of water which she dashed on the hapless boy's head. Daddy renewed his loud conversation with the Lord, informing his maker in cacophonous tones that chances of his ever living to see another birthday were slim to none. (He said a lot more, but that was the general gist of the talk.) I, knowing full well who would have to clean up the kitchen after all the fuss blew over, had another helping of fried rabbit, with biscuits and jelly on the side.

After what seemed like an hour but in all probability was just a minute or two, the cold water on the head took effect and Reg began to come around. He tried, unsuccessfully I'm afraid, to explain what had happened, but his voice was simply gone from the prolonged screaming. It was several days before we pieced the whole story together.

Reg had gone hunting that afternoon after getting in from school, and sundown found him in an unfamiliar area of the woods. After trying what he hoped might be a shortcut, he became hopelessly lost and so made the sensible decision to wait for help instead of stumbling blindly through the darkening forest. In their early years, hill children are instructed as to survival in the woods, and Reg set about following the advice. He gathered a supply of fallen limbs and started to build a fire, relax, and wait for the help which he expected to come when he didn't get home by late bedtime.

Let me say at this point that Reg was not an overly imaginative child; neither was he given to gross exaggeration, as was Bert, in order to make a point. I cannot explain what happened.

Just before he struck the match to light his fire, Reg declared, he heard a soft, low, mystifying chuckle coming from the woods behind him. His first, rather pleasant thought was that Bert had already come to his rescue and was just providing a little extra thrill to the situation by impersonating "Raw Head and Bloody Bones." ("RH&BB," our personal creation, was a ghoulish monster who lurked somewhere deep in the wilds, waiting to steal lost children, smear them all over with lard so they would easily slide down his throat, and swallow them whole! We often lulled ourselves to sleep by telling one another horrible stories about him, and Mama wondered why Clark had such terrible nightmares.)

Reg was just ready to call out to his brother that he was not fooled when the sound was repeated directly in front of him, and this time it was considerably louder. His hair began to come uncombed in its effort to stand up straight, and his skin not only crawled, it seemed to want to run.

Rapidly he reevaluated the opinion of being teased by his brother. Reg knew that Bert, though his faults were many, was still a human being, and the sound which filled his soul with deep, numbing terror could not have been brought forth from a mortal.

He was a brave child, but fear took over completely when he heard the high, sobbing pseudo-laughter for the third time. His hardy spirit cracked and the race was on.

Daddy later walked back to the scene of the event, which wasn't all that far from home. He reported that so far as he could determine, Reggie's initial strides measured about eight feet apart, narrowing down to just under seven as he got closer home. He had really cut a wide swath through the underbrush, as the numerous cuts and gashes on his face attested.

As luck would have it, Reg was headed in the right direction when he started his night run. No telling when or where we would have found him had he been pointed in the wrong way.

Daddy always felt that the "thing" was a mother fox

protecting her young. Vixens could make very unusual sounds, he told us, when trying to frighten enemies away from their den. (Reg acknowledged that if such was the case, the mother fox had met with phenomenal success!)

Most of the neighborhood thought it was an old panther out on the prowl, and Reg was known for years as "the boy that outran the last known devil cat in Oregon County!"

My theory at the time, and I have never had reason to change my mind, was that he had unquestionably found "Raw Head and Bloody Bones" himself. Reg was just lucky that "RH&BB" happened to have run out of lard.

None of us ever teased him much about the experience, and that was not like us. Normally we tormented each other unmercifully at the slightest opportunity.

Whatever the "thing" was, the boy had truly been out of his mind with fear and it was not funny to any of us at the time.

And it's not funny to Reg to this very day!

Chapter 11

THE HANGING

Unfortunately, Daddy found the remains of the suicide before we could finalize our funeral plans and get the deceased underground. As we expected, his reaction to the loss was pretty bad. "God help us all!" he screamed in the direction of paradise. "I don't know what in the hell is going to happen around here next!"

Try as I may, I cannot recall how we obtained our beloved pet goat, Billy Waddles, but I had nightmares for years over the way we lost him. This wonderful little animal was a great addition to our family of pets for the brief period of time he was with us. We bathed him, brushed his hair, tied ribbons onto his ears, and hunted him down with a vengeance when he would run away.

His habit of leaving home was the biggest problem we ever had with Billy. He seemed to have a special feeling for our neighbors up the hill, Dr. and Mrs. Burch. When he could escape our loving attention, he visited them. One day Mrs. Burch opened her door, not knowing Billy was on the porch, and in he walked, looked around, and went over to lie down by the china cabinet, completely at home.

This tendency to hunt for greener pastures caused the charming little goat to meet his Waterloo, for in an effort to discourage his straying off and bothering folks, one of us decided to tie him to a tree for the night. This proved to be an extremely bad idea.

In the late evening hours, the feeling of restraint got to be too much for Billy. Being a goat, he started running and jumping. As he circled the tree, the rope became shorter and shorter, and when he attemped to vault the low limb to which he was tied, the results were neck-breaking!

When we found him the next morning, it was terrible beyond description. There he hung, cold as kraut, tongue and eyes protruding grotesquely, his tiny ears still colorfully decorated with the red, white, and blue ribbons dating back to the Fourth of July celebration.

We restrained our grief as best we could until Daddy left for work, because we didn't want him to know about the tragedy. (We figured if we could get the funeral out of the way before dinnertime, as the noon meal is called in the hill country, he would never miss the goat. Daddy was not a fool about our pets and tended to ignore them most of the time, except for the cats. He hated cats, and they knew to stay out of the way of his feet.)

As soon as the old truck pulled out of the driveway that morning, we called the Jones kids down and began making funeral plans. Their family and ours had a large turnover of pets, and through the years we had become truly adept at providing a good service for the deceased animals. It seemed to assuage our grief somewhat to put the dearly departed away nicely.

Millard Henry, younger brother to Stealy, had a powerful voice for a small child and usually played the part of the minister, while the girls of the Jones family, Carlene and Nita, who both had lovely voices, would sing a medley of sorrowful songs. "Precious Memories" was one of our all-time favorites, and they could be depended upon to do it really well.

Unfortunately, we spent the entire morning in just the planning and preparation stages for the last rites of Billy. When we heard Daddy's truck chugging up the hill at dinnertime, we realized we had held the body too long!

Now Billy was a pretty big animal, and we had no good place close to hide the corpse. (We hadn't gotten very far along on digging the grave.) We could only watch and tremble while Daddy came over to view the remains.

Sure enough. He exploded! (Daddy...not Billy.)

Calling the rest of the family to the grave-side, he shrieked, "Don't you know...don't you blithering idiots know that goats jump over limbs? It is the very nature of the animals to jump! God help me that I should live to see the day when a child of mine would be so sadly lacking in common sense as to tie a goat to a tree with a rope!!"

Frothy flecks of spittle collected in the corners of his mouth, and small veins jumped in his temple as he made his closing remarks, "As God is my witness, this is the end and I'm through with the lot of you imbeciles! Through... do you hear me? THROUGH!!!"

Daddy was not a person to mince words when he was angry.

Mama, showing deep emotion, was holding the baby, Iris, who was too small to realize what was taking place. It seemed rather strange to watch the little one laughing and cooing while the rest of us were enduring such a verbal assault. Mama kept saying, through her tears, that she did hope none of the neighbors could hear Daddy talking like that, but of course they could since none of them were totally deaf.

Normally, after such an outburst Daddy calmed down rather quickly, but it was several days following the interment before we were allowed back in the house.

We spent a lot of time that week with the Jones kids.

Chapter 12

DING, DONG, BELL!
WHAT THE HELL IS IN THE WELL?

It was not at all unusual for our family to have company back in the thirties. Times were hard and the Depression was deep. Lots of folks were moving about in search of employment, and Mama and Daddy did not turn anyone away. Certainly they were not alone in this open door policy, since feeding those unable to provide for themselves was a big part of "the code of the hills" by which we were brought up. If we had food, we shared with those who did not.

A number of our visitors were city people, and small town living seemed to hold a deep fascination for them, especially for the children who had "grown up on the sidewalks," as Mama said.

Since we lived outside the city limits, we did not have access to the municipal water supply and were dependent on a deep well in the back yard to furnish our needs. This underground reservoir never failed to fascinate visiting city kids, who felt we were indeed fortunate to have such an interesting natural resource on our own place. In order to obtain the water which lay some hundred feet or so below ground level, it was necessary to pull a long, skinny bucket out of a long, skinny pipe, and we were more than happy to share this unparalleled experience with our guests.

At the time of which I write the family sharing our home was equipped with three children, two of school age and a baby about three. This smallest one seemed inordinately fond of taking in the operation of the well. He seized every opportunity to peer into the small well opening which, when not in use, was covered with a small, rusty bucket that fitted quite snugly (or so we thought) over the exposed well pipe.

The little fellow seemed equally fascinated with the numerous puppies which populated our yard. Daddy, being a "fox huntin' man," prided himself not a little on having some of the best hounds in our part of the state. Our small visitor was seldom seen without one of the multitudinous pups clutched tightly to his bosom, its bulging eyes attesting to a slow demise from lack of oxygen. We found one he had loved to death!

He got rid of another one, too.

It would appear that the child was familiar with the nursery rhyme, "Ding, Dong, Bell. Pussy's in the Well," and one hot afternoon he decided to act out the part of "Little Johnny Green."

Not having a cat available was no deterrent; he simply picked up Little Smokey as a suitable substitute. (Little Smokey was the pup on which Daddy pinned his hopes of winning another bench and field trial trophy.) Now you must realize that the pup was fat and the pipe was narrow, and how the child managed to cram his sacrifice into the opening we were unable to determine. Perhaps he poked it down with the hoe handle. I don't know how he did it, but he accomplished his mission.

When Daddy got home from work that evening his first thought was for a cold drink of water. We kids were supposed to keep the water bucket full, but of course we didn't. Mama always said if the house caught on fire she'd grab the bucket because it would be the first thing to burn. (Mama had some inspired moments of rhetorical brilliance.)

Muttering obscenities to himself, Daddy seized the empty bucket and hurried to the back yard, where he attemped to hurl the long, narrow well bucket into the narrow opening. (It was in no way necessary to "hurl" the well bucket, but he was mad.) The bucket refused to cooperate. It did not permit itself to be lowered into the well.

When Daddy realized the bucket was hitting an obstacle he was bewildered and considered the possibility that the metal casing might be caving in, as sometimes happened in old wells. After making several attempts to lower the bucket, he noticed our small boarder smiling benignly, fat pup in arms, and pointing a chubby little finger at the well.

"Dear God, NO!! IT CAN'T BE!!" our father screamed as he realized what was so effectively hindering his attempts to obtain water. "Tell me, Dear Lord, tell me that blithering idiot has not stuffed a pup in my well!!"

The divine conversation intensified as it continued, and Mama, crying softly, herded us kids to the front yard. Several of the neighbors, drawn by the one-sided dialogue between Daddy and the Almighty, came over and we children were gradually dispatched throughout the community until the situation calmed somewhat. We were more than reluctant to leave the excitement.

When we got back home (we ate supper with the neighbors) the visitors had packed up and moved on. They did not leave a forwarding address, and we never heard from them anymore, not even at Christmas.

It was a big mess getting the pup fished out of the well. I am not going to try to describe that procedure.

Our family didn't return to a state even resembling normality for weeks. Daddy was deeply troubled with bad dreams for a long time, sometimes waking the household with soft moans and an intermittent question directed towards heaven, "Why me, Lord, why me?"

For years following the incident he searched the papers, especially after a particularly heinous crime, and swore that he wouldn't be a damned bit surprised if the jibbering imbecile who had thrown his dog down the well wasn't responsible for most of the crime done in the state of Missouri! I do believe Daddy was a bit disappointed that we never knew the child to be hailed before the justices.

And he never was able to accept the fact that somehow, just accidentally, out of a whole yard of dogs, the idiot had disposed of the pick of the litter.

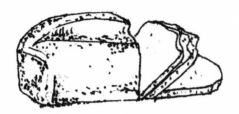

Chapter 13

GOOD TIMES WITH GOOD MAMA

Good Mama got the name from my sister, Anne, who was one of her oldest grandchildren. Nothing we could have called our grandmother would have been more appropriate, for this cherished little lady was "good" in every sense of the word. And she was a pure delight to be around. One of the highlights of summer vacation was the week or two each of us got to spend with her and Good Papa on their farm. She made those days memorable.

How she loved to laugh! She could tell jokes with the best wit in the country. "Preacher" stories were her favorites and, being a born-again Methodist, she nearly always involved the Baptist denomination in a rather negative but loving way.

One of her good ones started, "Now I guess I really shouldn't tell this story, seein' it's about a Baptist preacher, but the Lord will forgive me and who cares if the Baptists do or not."

She continued, "One day there was this Baptist

preacher who was so lazy he couldn't even support lice! His congregation had just about got fed up with takin' care of his family, so they got together and come up with a plan to scare him into goin' to work. Sent him word they were gonna hang him, he was just too triflin' to live, and they tied him up, put him in a wagon, and started off to the hangin' tree.

"Now they had it planned out good. 'Bout halfway there, they had a fella ride up and offer to help the preacher out if the congregation would change their mind about the hangin'. Said he'd give him a whole wagon load of corn. The lazy preacher raised up from the wagon and asked, 'Is the corn shelled?' and when the fella told him it was still on the cob, the sorry son of a gun laid back down and said, 'Drive on...drive on.' "

I'll bet she's been telling jokes on the Baptists ever since she got to heaven!

When Good Mama was raising her family, pie suppers were social events not to be missed unless someone in the household was awaiting death or the birth of a child. These affairs, in which young men made bids on the pastries created by their girlfriends, were sponsored by charitable organizations such as graveyard maintenance societies, women's unions against the evils of alcohol, and other institutions of mercy. (Seems more fun to me than our present policy of accosting the traveling public at stop signs. One of these days I'm liable to run over some half-nude kid with a tin can.)

Being as lazy as allowed, Good Mama's lovely daughters (and Mama was one of them) would always beg her to make the pies, which they would pass off as their own creations. The girls preferred spending their time decorating the box or basket which would contain the suc-culent pastry created by their mother's loving hands.

Piney School was hosting the pie supper on the night of which I write. The desserts had been purchased by each special boyfriend, and the young people had paired off to begin the process of cutting and serving the pie. Suddenly Mama burst into tears of embarrassment! (Even in her youth she cried easily.) When her beau cut through the beautifully browned, piled high meringue, he encountered plain, old corn bread, cold as kraut and hard as a rock!

Good Mama laughed until she cried before bringing out the real pastry.

And that is not the end of my recollections of her monkeyshines.

During my vacation weeks at the farm, I loved to help her make yeast bread. No small part of the fun lay in the unique method we came up with for kneading the bread, which was to play pitch and catch with the large wad of dough. (We didn't drop it very often, but if such a mishap occurred, we just mixed the dirt and dust into the sticky mass and no one was ever the wiser. Seems to me that back then folks didn't worry a lot about germs; too busy trying to make a living, I guess.)

Now in order to finish my story, I must tell you that my grandfather was not the world's bravest man. He was in no way ashamed of this craven streak and did not try to conceal it. The supernatural was very real to him, and he could scare the daylights out of us all (including himself) telling ghost stories. He took a rather unusual pride in declaring most emphatically that he would no more have spent a night alone in his home than he would have robbed a bank and shot the teller. (Nowadays we would say he was your basic coward.)

One of the many things which caused him to come apart at the seams was any object even remotely resembling a snake. Good Mama knew this and one morning, while in the midst of bread making, she came up with a plan which would capitalize on this weakness. (As I told you, my grandmother loved a good joke and would labor mightily to pull one off.)

Our plot could not have been more simple. We formed a "snake" of sorts from bread dough and gave it a good coating of black shoe polish. The strange creature was topped off with black button eyes and placed just off the path Good Papa would walk when he came home for his noon meal.

This was summertime, remember, and the hot July sun was beating down when my grandpa started from the cornfield to the house for dinner. (We call the noon meal "dinner" in the hill country.) When the first wild, maniacal scream blasted the tranquility of the kitchen we knew he had spied our creation.

Good Mama and I ran out of the house to enjoy the fruits of our joke, and when we saw the results of our artistry we just fell to the ground laughing. The summer sun had caused our dough sculpture to swell to enormous proportions. The shoe polish had been greatly enhanced by the leavening action of the yeast, and the final result looked a whole lot like a gigantic copperhead snake.

It took us quite awhile to get Good Papa calmed down. He did not join in our merriment and took a different path home for several weeks.

Wouldn't you have to love practical jokes to go to all that trouble?

Chapter 14

SLIM PICKINGS

Recently I read a report which indicated that years ago hoboes developed a method of marking a particular dwelling which proved sympathetic to their needs. I believe it! For a time during the Depression we lived fairly close to a highway, and many days we had more than one of the unfortunates drop by, wanting to do odd jobs for a meal. Almost everyone along the road tried to feed them because they were usually young boys actively seeking work, and we never knew when some member of our own family might need help of a similar nature.

It was really no big deal to provide food because almost always there was something which could be brought out for these needy folks. Mama cooked three meals a day from "scratch," a term we didn't recognize at that time since mixes had not hit the market as yet. Well do I remember, VERY well do I remember the first time Mama utilized a "mix" to put a chocolate cake on the table. Unfortunately, Daddy found the empty box in the trash, and never at a loss for words, he began to take her to task for trying to bring down the health of his children with food not fit to be consumed by the hogs. (That is a direct quote.)

"Great God Almighty, Clair!" he screamed. "Don't you ever read the papers? Four families in Arkansas were wiped out just last week, totally and completely wiped out, from eating such foul poison as you have put on the table for these innocent children to eat!!" (If I remember correctly, it was ptomaine that got the folks in Arkansas, but Daddy never hesitated to circumvent the truth in order to make his point.)

He ended his tirade by informing the entire neighborhood that if God had meant cakes to come out of boxes, He would never have seen fit to make Mama such a good cook. By the time his exhortation was finished, we kids had eaten all the cake, and he was unable to personally verify the baseness of products found in cardboard boxes. (Later in life, Daddy mellowed somewhat and even sank so low as to drink instant coffee, though he never admitted to liking it at all.)

But I digress.

One late afternoon, a young man knocked on the back door and politely asked if there was any work he might do in exchange for something to eat. On this occasion Mama was mightily embarrassed, because we had finished dinner and I do mean finished! Nothing had been left except a large quantity of corn bread; no sweet milk, no fried potatoes, no cherry cobbler, not even a smidgen of butter or jelly remained. Every bite of food had been consumed except for the corn bread, and it was cold and rather dried out by then.

There was, however, setting on the work table in the corner, a big crock of clabbered milk waiting to be poured into an old pillowcase and hung on the clothesline. There it would slowly drip until all the whey was on the ground, and the remaining curds would magically be transformed by Mama into delicious cottage cheese. But at that time it was nothing but awful, old, sour milk, enough to turn the stoutest stomach.

Mama explained to the young man that she had only the corn bread and milk, thinking he would go on to the next place for a better meal, but he said, "Lady, I'm hungry. I'm real hungry, and that sounds mighty good to me."

And he ate all that cold corn bread, stirring it into the sour milk and eating it as we would have eaten cereal. Then he thanked Mama most politely and left. (The men never failed to thank her for the humble meals they received and the meals were humble, because we were living very close to the edge of poverty.)

Mama said later that was the most extreme case she had to deal with. Miss Pearlie Maxine maintained that FDR got the country straightened out shortly thereafter.

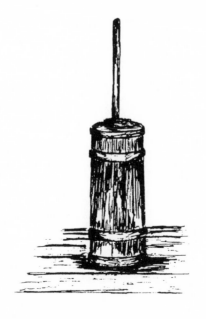

Chapter 15

HOME REMEDIES, OR HOW TO KILL YOURSELF WITHOUT REALLY TRYING!

Small children didn't receive a whole lot of medical attention during my growing up years. As far as that goes, adults didn't either. I remember being at the farm one summer when Good Mama was unfortunate enough to step on a nail while we were picking up kindling around the barn. The wound became infected, and it was truly an evil sight with streaks of red radiating from the puncture.

So Good Papa, utilizing his vast knowledge of folk medicine, undertook to cure her by making a poultice of warm cow manure with a few fried onions thrown in to ensure success. Using a flour sack for a bandage, he tied that corrupt, smelly, vile mess of so-called medication onto my grandmother's foot.

Good Mama, being a hearty soul, not only survived the treatment but even made a speedy recovery, possibly to rid herself of the awful remedy.

Later that summer she got her revenge when Good Papa was taken violently ill with stomach cramps in the middle of the night. Not being given to suffering in silence (as is true with most men, I have found), he woke us with moans and groans which rapidly accelerated to wild screams of agony. (I always thought he was "puttin' on" a lot and milking his discomfort for all it was worth.)

In order to save his life without having to call the doctor, Good Mama had me help her strip the little peach tree in the backyard almost bare of foliage. After building a fire in the stove, she boiled the green leaves into a sticky, gooey concoction and slapped it (still steaming!) onto my grandfather's wretched stomach.

As you might guess, this action did little, if anything, to diminish the intensity of his cries. Yet he, also, survived this extreme therapy, though it seemed to me he was considerably weakened by the experience for several days.

Nearly every time I open a flip-top can of soda I am reminded of an injury I stupidly inflicted upon myself. Occasionally Daddy would bring home a carton of Cokes for us to share, and I was always first in line for mine. In those days special openers had to be used on soda, and since none of us were very good about putting kitchen utensils back in the proper drawer after using them, our opener was nearly always misplaced.

That didn't stop me. I developed an alternate method which not only allowed me to get to the Coke, but it also slowed my consumption, permitting me to enjoy the drink for a longer time. (Please notice: I do NOT recommend this procedure.)

Securing the bottle firmly in my left hand, I would jab a hole all the way through the metal cap with an ice pick and then drink the Coke as it slowly dripped through the small puncture. (By the time I finished the soda was usually very warm.)

As any fool would know, eventually this practice proved

to be dangerous. One evening when I made the stab, my aim wasn't good and instead of piercing the bottle cap, the ice pick went through two of my fingers (curled as they were around the bottle) and into the third. Fortunately, the pick missed the bones, but there I was, my fingers a shish kebab neatly secured on an ice pick.

Excitedly, the other kids crowded around, shoving and pushing, to enjoy such a sight, unusual even in our household. Anne told me if I'd pull the skewer out by myself she wouldn't tell Mama, who in all probability would have a crying fit.

I pulled it out, and she didn't tell on me. As I recall, my fingers were not even sore. Perhaps it was mind over matter. I sure didn't want a cow manure poultice!

But the worst injury of my life happened in an even more unusual way.

One summer, shortly after school was over, my Girl Scout troop planned a cookout, and it fell my lot to provide potatoes for the meal. We grew our own vegetables, of course, and kept them in a cellar under the house. Even when a child, I was about as clumsy as a pregnant cow, and climbing out of the cellar I slipped on the wooden steps, fell hard, and literally knocked a big hole in my leg, just below the knee.

The force of the blow must have numbed my leg because I felt no pain as I started hunting some family member other than Mama to give me first aid. (Being the chubby child that I was, a large amount of yellow fat oozed from the wound, and what with the bone being clearly visible, I felt that Mama would probably go all to pieces at the sight. She did not handle emergencies too well, and we tried to protect her as much as possible.)

Fortunately, I stumbled across Daddy before anyone else saw me, and he took immediate action. Cursing profusely, and laughing a bit to keep me from being scared, he started gathering what medical supplies he could find.

As luck would have it, there was an ample supply of bichloride of mercury disinfectant tablets left from some do-it-yourself surgery Daddy had performed on one of the hounds which were so plentiful around our place. (I believe the operation had been on Old Smokey, who had the misfortune of getting caught in a barbed wire fence. The resulting wound caused an amputation to be required and Daddy did it himself. No unnecessary vet bills for him.)

Anyway, Old Smokey had made it without any problems, so I got the same treatment, except Daddy didn't amputate my leg above the knee. I survived but my leg was a mess all summer. Still, I took it better than Mama did. She was in bed for days.

Ironically, the very next day Reg fell and laid his knee open in much the same fashion. He got the same treatment. Although our parents didn't believe in pampering youngsters, I think Daddy was deeply concerned at the injuries for I recall him saying, "You kids will carry these scars to your graves."

He was right, too. The incident took place fifty years ago, and the scar still mars my otherwise lovely leg. I have always had a gut level feeling that the ugly imperfection kept me from being nominated for Mrs. America. Maybe not.

Chapter 16

SPARE THE ROD

Numerous and great are the changes which have come about since the growing up days of my youth, but I'd like to bet my last dollar that nothing has altered more through the years than the discipline of children.

Mama and Daddy tried to raise us right, and both of them totally embraced the Biblical advice that "to spare the rod is to spoil the child." They interpreted the Scripture to read "lay it on!"'

Mama didn't like to hit us unless she was terribly disturbed, and her favorite means of controlling the tribe was to shriek at the top of her voice, "Just you wait till your daddy gets home! I'll have him tend to you with his BELT!"

One day Iris had been caught in some horrendous offense and Mama assured her it would be reported "when your daddy gets home." (If memory serves me, Iris had been caught eavesdropping on the neighbor ladies who had gathered in the back yard to help Mama peel peaches.

Deep discussions of sexual and obstetrical problems were held at such times, and about all the education we ever received in this area was gleaned from such summer conversations. We especially looked forward to visits from Miss Lizzie Schmidt, who was quite hard of hearing which meant, naturally, that the other ladies had to talk loud. Really loud. From our hiding places behind the house we could hear every word regarding protracted labor, retained afterbirth, and many other gruesome problems of a childbearing nature. Not one of us believed the stork brought babies.)

But I digress.

When Mama made her disciplinary report to the head of the house that evening, Iris was instructed to step into the bedroom, and when Daddy pulled off the BELT, she felt her time on earth might possibly be limited. He just grinned at her and said, "Now sweetheart, when I hit the bed, you holler as loud as you can and we'll fool your mother." Needless to say, Iris was happy to enter into the conspiracy.

After three hard licks, and the accompanying screams, Mama yelled, "That's enough, Willard. Supper's gettin' cold."

Iris laughs about that to this day.

Good behavior was not to be left at home, either. One of my earliest recollections is of Daddy giving instructions as to what he expected while we were at our educational institution. Each fall, right before school started, he would introduce the subject at the supper table. In a manner not at all gentle, the directions started. "If there's anything on God's green earth I can't stomach, it's a smart-alecky kid, and I'm tellin' each and every one of you that all your teachers have my permission to slap you out of your chair if you're ever disrespectful to them!"

Looking back, I know that Daddy would have physically attacked anyone who "slapped us out of our chair," but we didn't know it then. And while the threat didn't make us very good, it did make us very careful. We certainly couldn't take a chance on the teachers telling of our misdeeds because he continued his orders with, "And another thing you'd better remember. If you get a paddlin' at school, you can be blamed sure you'll get another one twice as hard when you get home. God knows your mother and I have tried to raise you right, and I'll not have you disgracin' this family by misbehavin' at school!"

This general conversation, with additions and deletions, took place each year, and woe unto any one of us who failed to remember the dire consequences of rambuntiousness in the educational process.

Our parents never seemed to worry a lot about the damage such a vitriolic tirade might have on a small child's psyche; indeed, they were probably not aware that such a problem existed. And let me say right here they never lost a great deal of sleep wondering if we might grow up hating them and all other authority figures.

So far as I can tell, being made to behave ourselves (and I use the term rather loosely) never caused any severe trauma to any of us, and we have become decent, respected, citizens of our communities. We all pay taxes, though we don't like to anymore than you do, and no one in the family has ever fallen afoul of the law, other than that one incident involving an armored car. Neither have we been driven to drugs or drink, unless you are ridiculously conservative and count beer and whiskey.

Chapter 17

JACK SPRAT COULD EAT NO FAT!
AND HE WAS NOT ALONE

You might think with a big family such as ours we would eat anything that stayed on the plates, but such was not the case. Indeed, no! Such was not the case at all. Although we were fervent partakers of the dishes we especially enjoyed, we had several idiosyncrasies peculiar and unique to us alone.

For instance, any one of us would have been far more willing to chew up and swallow a live toad than to permit a single morsel of fat meat to enter our mouths. Clark used to take a long time at breakfast crumbling bacon and rolling it through his fingers several times to ensure that no stray shred of fat might be left to foul his digestive tract. Only a minuscule amount of lean would remain to eat with his biscuit and jelly, but that was alright with him. It wasn't fat.

Since it was rather expensive we didn't have steak very often, and we all looked forward to the occasions when it graced our table. Strangers eating with us were seldom able to identify the meat because Mama had developed her own, distinctive method of preparing the delicacy.

First, she would trim every morsel of fat from the thick slices of round steak. With the edge of a saucer, she then pounded flour, salt, and pepper into the meat. (This process of hammering took place until she gave out.) Finally, she fried the remains in about an inch of hot bacon grease for thirty-five minutes or until it resembled the sole of an old shoe, whichever came first. And you know what? That is the only way we would eat steak!

To this very day, I cut off every visible sign of the marbling which Speedy vows enhances the flavor of a wonderful T-bone steak. Not to me it doesn't! and it never will! Old habits die hard with us hill folks.

Mama treated ham the same way. Remember that flavorful, smoke-cured, mouth-watering treat of yesteryear? She fried it till the cows came home! The chewing process was lengthy, but we liked it that way. (Good Papa, who had a shoe last and did minor cobbling for us, swore he could half-sole a shoe with our leftover ham.)

But eggs were the biggest challenge we had to face. Since a few chickens were always running around the yard Mama had a lot of eggs to use in cooking, and occasionally she fried some for breakfast. It was difficult to get them cooked done enough for any of us, because we wanted them fried HARD!

A heavy, iron spatula was used in breakfast preparations, and with it Mama turned eggs into black, flat, tough, lacy-looking vulcanized rubber. Any chance of nutritional value remaining was slim to none. We used sharp knives to cut them, and Iris had the debatable honor of being the only child in school to have broken a tooth on a fried egg.

You know what? We all still eat them like that!

Indeed, since all of us ate "eggs a la cremation" (a descriptive phrase coined by my husband the first time he saw me prepare one for personal consumption), none of us knew our eating habits to be unusual. Iris informed us of the ways of the outside world concerning eggs after she returned from a hound-hunting trip with Daddy. She was deeply shaken by the experience.

One Sunday they embarked on a quest for a foxhound which had been lost on a recent hunt. After searching for the dog all morning without results, the two of them arrived at a friend's house way, way back in the hills, about noontime. These hospitable folks insisted they join them at the table for dinner, as the mid-day meal is called in the hill country.

Guess what was on the menu! You got it. A huge platter of wide-eyed, greasy, soft-cooked eggs nestled on top of thick, pink, partially cooked slabs of ham. Great, disgusting, nauseating gobs of tepidly-warm, white fat loosely clung to the offensive mess of meat.

The crowning insult to Iris's stomach was a generous bowl of cream gravy, a dish completely foreign to her. (Her original thought, when first viewing the food, was that somehow wallpaper paste had found its way onto the table. Gravy was never prepared in our home because the very thought of ingesting such an obscenity made Daddy grievously ill. The very word was evil to him, ranking right up alongside abortion and infant baptism. It probably does not come as much of a shock to you that we did not put anything on the table which Daddy found unpleasant.) As the diners started passing the food around, a rooster walked in the kitchen door (which did not have a screen to prevent fowl excursions of this type), and he flew onto the table to peck at the biscuits. Unhappily, they were located at my sister's elbow. Iris was unaccustomed to chickens on the table, and it shocked her not a little.

She looked at Daddy. He tried to smile. It was a failure. They both knew there was no way in the world, short of physical torture, that either of them could permit that grossness to be placed upon their plates, yet the "code of the hills" would not allow them to leave the hospitality of a friend's house without a token meal being eaten.

Iris did the only thing possible under the circumstances (and being a weak-stomached child, it was not difficult). Her breakfast was returned in the most unpleasant way you can possibly imagine.

Seizing the golden opportunity, Daddy jumped to his feet and began castigating himself for bringing his small child out of the house while she was still recovering from a severe case of chicken-pox. (The Cash family can think fast when faced with having to eat almost raw eggs and fat meat!) He told his friends he was certainly sorry for all the trouble and for them to be sure to stop by the next time they came to town.

The search for the lost hound was over for the day. On the way home, Daddy congratulated Iris on saving them from a fate worse than death. They drove fast, almost thirty miles an hour, because they were getting awfully hungry and wanted to be home by suppertime.

Chapter 18

THE DIRTY HALF DOZEN

Do you remember when you could go into a grocery store and pull off as many bananas as you wanted from a stalk which hung suspended from the ceiling?

When you could buy so much cheese and crackers for a dime that you were not able to eat it all for lunch and would end up feeding it to the town stray?

When anyone who "ran a bill" at the local market (and nearly everyone did back then) was given a large sack of candy as a reward for paying up at the end of the month?

When this same market would deliver grocery needs to the home, twice a day, even if all you wanted was a can of pork 'n' beans or a loaf of bread?

When you could buy a cup of coffee for a nickel and a large slab of pie for a dime at the White Kitchen Cafe?

When coffee cans opened with a key and creative ladies saved the metal spirals which resulted when the tops were removed to hang on their Christmas trees?

When small children were not allowed to assault the

elderly in their efforts to be first in line?

When you could go to a movie for a dime but you seldom had a dime?

When parents were not fearful for their children to roam the streets and play all over town so long as they were home by suppertime?

When sex education was not that high on the list of priorities and for females consisted of the three words, "JUST SAY NO!"

When oranges and lemons were individually wrapped in tissue paper, usually deep blue in color, and creative people saved it to make Christmas tree ornaments?

And that brings me to the subject of this story.

Some of my school friends (unnatural youths for the time), made use of these cast-off tissues for another, less praiseworthy purpose, I'm afraid. These boys, semi-imbeciles, mean, ornery, and proud of it to the point of calling themselves "The Dirty Half Dozen," developed the following scheme.

They held no love for our superintendent of schools, who was a fine, upstanding Christian man, though somewhat unusual for our area in that he was of German origin and was Republican in political persuasion. (Oregon County has never been a stronghold of the GOP, to say the very least.)

One of the boys, J.P. Le Fluer, accompanied by the five other village idiots, purloined a large cardboard box from his father, who had the little store across from school. The group then carefully covered the bottom of the container with what I can only describe as a pungent and plentiful by-product of the Farm Animal Sales Barn. On top of the fresh fertilizer, to hide it from sight as well as to serve as fuel, they put dozens of the bright, blue tissues which had originally contained citrus fruit.

88

Under cover of darkness they marched proudly past the funeral home to deposit their unique creation on the front porch of our educational leader, Mr. Mueller.

The plot had been carefully worked out. When the designated arsonist torched the box, another dimwit rang the doorbell, leaving the remaining simpletons to run like crazy to their pre-allotted hiding places. Mr. Mueller came to answer the doorbell in his house shoes, having mistakenly thought himself settled in for the night. Becoming extremely upset upon viewing the bonfire on his front porch, he immediately endeavored to stomp out the conflagration. This led to a remarkably untidy situation, in which both his house shoes and lower limbs were liberally splattered with cow manure.

The boys laughed until they cried, rolling around on the grass, not even troubling to stifle their howls of mirth, because Mr. Mueller was extremely hard of hearing and did not have his mechanical aid in at the time. As I said, he had erroneously thought himself retired for the night, and the hearing aid was resting on his night stand.

The boys had the gall to present their victim with a pair of scuffs at Christmas time, though one of them did have limited intelligence enough to insist they not sign their names to the gift.

So far as I know, the group was never brought to law for the ugly act, and unless you count the one who became a member of the U.S. Senate, they all ended up decent, hard-working, tax-paying citizens. Needless to say, the whole community was surprised at this baffling turn of events.

Chapter 19

THE PREACHER AND THE SPARE

Recreation, like just about everything else, was totally homemade during the thirties and for as long as I can remember, hunting and hound dogs loomed large in the leisure time activities of our clan. Many summer nights, and always on Saturday evening, some member of the family could be found helping Daddy load the pack of foxhounds, his pride and joy, into the back of our old pickup truck.

After checking to see that he had his horn for calling the dogs in when the hunt was over, he'd be off to pick up a few buddies. With their choicest dogs (and a little bottle of moonshine in case of snake bite), the group would be off to the deep woods until the wee hours of morning. Sometimes daybreak saw them in.

Fox hunting, as explained to me, has nothing to do with catching a fox, only the chasing of it by the dogs, while the waiting men listen to the "run" and identify individual hounds by their baying. (Daddy told of one idiot from the city who thought the hunters would run madly through the woods, following the dogs until they captured the fox. Cletus Lumley had to be physically restrained when he heard the imbecile express that opinion of the hunt. "Nobody that stupid oughta be allowed to live in the world with the rest of us." Cletus remarked as he started to the truck after his gun.)

It was pleasant for the hunters to sit around the campfire, smoke, drink, and discuss the physical attributes of Bobbie Jo Bilderback, our town's answer to Jean Harlow.

It always seemed to me that some element of sport lay in convincing the womenfolks that the hunt was of prime importance to the health of both man and beast. Thus, the men argued, it should completely override such inconsequential and mundane things as a low woodpile in the winter and imminent childbirth in the fall. (When we were older, Daddy justified his summer absences by reminding us that Mama always started looking for the new baby in March or April, and it never made an appearance until September. He felt certain he would not miss out on the blessed event.)

One of the wives became so upset with the continued evening absences of her hunting husband that she was overheard (with no trouble at all!) to scream, "If you leave here tonight, don't bother to come back and look for me and these kids. I'm gonna pack up what I can carry and leave, do you hear me, leave!"

Late in the evening the man remarked to his friends that it just took a little something out of the hunt to know he was going home to an empty house.

These were dedicated hunters, make no mistake about it.

One of the faithful crew on Saturday night outings was

our minister, who was almost as devoted to his hunting hobby as he was to his calling to the ministry. As a general rule, fox hunters were not noted for restricted, demure, and ladylike conversation around the campfire, and most loved to "bend an elbow" several times in the course of an evening. Sometimes "the preacher," as he was respectfully known by his fellow sportsmen, had a lot to overlook. The men who were aware of his calling tried their best not to shock him because even those not professing to be Christians held his calling in high esteem, and would not have offended him for the world.

But now and then a stranger would come into their midst who did not know "the preacher" and embarrassing situations could and did arise.

Flat tires were a common problem in those days, and normally the equipment for patching tubes was carried in the back of all trucks, along with the other tools necessary for changing tires. But on one summer night the jack could not be found, and it looked as though the men would be very late getting to the woods after the flat occurred.

Luckily, a passing motorist was flagged down and the needed jack was borrowed. (It was not unusual for people to stop and help one another, since folks did not have to be afraid of everything that moved.)

The helper this evening was not aware of the clergyman in the group, and he began to loudly and frequently address his Creator in a manner not at all prayerful. Finally, it became so upsetting to the other men that someone called the "Good Samaritan" aside and informed him of the need to moderate his speech. The poor fellow almost cried from embarrassment and barely spoke during the completion of the task.

Later, when Daddy apologized to his friend for the

language which had been inflicted upon him, "the preacher" just grinned and said, "Willard, I can stand a little bit of cussin' if I know it's gonna help us get on with the hunt!"

Like I said, we are talking about dedication here.

Chapter 20

PUMP SPOUTS AND MOTH BALLS

Looking back through the mists of more than half a century, I can but marvel that Mama and Daddy retained any shreds of sanity at all after dealing with the problems of life brought about by a big family and an inadequate income.

For purposes of survival each of them developed totally different methods of coping with the tensions and frustrations of life.

Our parents had a lot to endure, and most of their trouble came from us kids. I offer the following events as fair examples.

At suppertime one cold winter evening Daddy entertained us with what he intended as a parable concerning a small child of his acquaintance. The little one, his classmate of many years ago, was so pitifully lacking in common sense as to put her tongue to the frosty spout of the schoolhouse pump. There she stuck, Daddy said, held firmly in place by her organ of communication until help arrived in the form of the teacher.

The removal process was a painful and bloody ordeal, Daddy told us sorrowfully, and he voiced the certain opinion that his offspring had more intelligence than to repeat this simple-minded tot's mistake.

Such was not the case, however.

Not long after, on a bitter, icy day, I felt compelled to verify the authenticity of Daddy's story. It didn't take an excessively long time to determine that, indeed, every word was true, and when my shrieks of pain and terror brought help in the form of my father, I knew myself to be in for more than a little verbal abuse.

And I was right!

"As God is my witness," he screamed, "I've produced an idiot! I told you...I TOLD YOU...why in the world can't you ever listen to a word I say? You gibbering imbecile...I TOLD YOU NOT TO STICK YOUR TONGUE TO A COLD PUMP!!!" And he yelled until he gave out.

That was one mistake I never repeated.

Mama's defensive mechanism was much more subtle. Today we would call it "laying on a guilt trip," but of course back then that terminology was unknown.

Mama was good at it. I've never seen anyone better. She could have made the saints feel a need to be born-again if she put her mind to it.

This is how it worked.

When one of us committed an offensive act Mama would sign heavily, cast her eyes towards heaven and intone in a voice which seemed to come from the depths of a tomb, "God knows you'll be sorry when you see me layin' in my coffin! And it won't do you any good to start cryin' then, 'cause it'll be too late, and I'll finally get some rest at last! You kids won't be able to drive me crazy anymore!" Then the tears would start flowing, and she would go on, and on, and on.

(Mama is hale and hearty, in her middle eighties now and enjoying better health than some of her offspring, though we don't say anything to her about it.)

When she hit her stride, she would start a review of all the past transgressions of the offender of the hour, and I must tell you she had a memory like an elephant. (Somehow she could cry all the while she talked. I guess it was some kind of special talent.)

Bert was an awfully mean kid and a terrible trial and tribulation to Mama. He was always doing such things as putting little rocks on the heating stove, and when they got really hot he'd slip them into someone's back pocket. Vicious things like that filled his days with joy. (Once he dropped a piece of ice down the baby's diaper. I have to admit it was terribly funny watching Iris try to crawl away from the chill. She couldn't figure out why it caught up with her every time she sat down.)

The entire family worried about Bert for a long time, fearful he would run afoul of the law, but our prayers were answered. He married a good woman who helped him to become a respectable, taxpaying citizen.

Anyway, one spring afternoon Mama was storing winter clothes in a large wooden chest, using a liberal sprinkling of moth balls to discourage the destructive insects from making a meal of our clothing. Bert, being inordinately fond of the smell of moth balls, was helping her in the task and wallowing in enjoyment of this plethora of wonderful odor!

(The only thing that kept me from making fun of the delight he found in the repulsive scent was that I like to smell skunks from a very far distance. May I say I get odd looks when I mention that quirk of my nature?)

Bert, always a resourceful child, conceived the idea of

getting nearer the object of his desire by pushing one moth ball up each nostril, thereby freeing his hands to help Mama while still enjoying the scent of the moth repellent at a close range.

Unfortunately, the pellets moved further up his olfactory organ than he had intended. When he tried to remove them he met with little success. Mama was notified of the problem and immediately became unglued, as was her habit. (I aways wondered why after so many years she didn't become hardened to any possible happening, but she never learned to slough off trouble.)

Mama always inhaled a deep breath of air before beginning her tirade, and when Bert saw her start to swell he perceived the rather obvious solution to his problem by inhaling a large amount of air and forcing it out his moth ball encumbered nose.

It worked quite well. When both moth balls hit the floor at the same time, the resulting noise was somewhat akin to a shotgun blast at close range. The child's hearing was slightly impaired for several weeks, but no long-range problems ensued.

Bert's interest in moth balls dwindled shortly thereafter, and he took up riding stick horses.

Remember, we were before tranquilizers.

Chapter 21

THE CALL OF THE CANYON

The lunch we had brought with us was magnificent, and I was tearing into my second chicken leg when Jessie remarked in a tone somewhat less than casual, "Martha, you know they're gonna beat us ta death if we get killed out here, don't 'cha?"

Even as a child I knew I was not genius material, but this remark seemed flawed even to my dull intellect. Seeking to comfort my companion, I answered, "Hey, they ain't ever gonna know 'bout it. Nobody saw us but them country folks, and we sure ain't gonna tell! 'Member how worried you wuz 'bout swimmin' in the sprang and we got outta that clean as a whistle."

The "sprang" was Mammoth Spring, a large body of icy water bordering Missouri and Arkansas, within easy walking distance of our home and the birthplace of summer pneumonia for countless generations of hill children. (It was a beautiful spot, a favorite parking place for lovers, and the moon's reflected likeness in the lovely lake spurred on many a teen-age romance. But this book is not an expose' so that is enough on the subject.)

I continued my words of reassurance, "You didn't sleep fer nearly a week and they still ain't found out. Least not yet."

"They," of course, referred to our parents who refused us permission to swim in the "sprang," not wanting to be out the money for expensive medical treatment. This was a time before penicillin, remember, and summer pneumonia was not to be taken lightly. Since the "sprang swimmin' " permission was denied, we knew our folks would never have given consent for the days outing had they known our destination to be the "Grand Gulf!"

In Oregon County, scene of my youth, a geological happening occurred some 450 million years ago which resulted in a series of large, underground passageways. As the millions of years passed, surface streams carved through the rock and soil and connected with the cave passages. In some areas the cave roof broke through and the stream was diverted underground. Now most of the roof has collapsed, probably within the past 10,000 years, geologists believe.

Today the Grand Gulf is a canyon three-fourths of a mile long with walls reaching as high as 120 feet. As you might imagine, this place of wonder was well-known to my generation of children. Quite often some of the young people would hike out to the site, a distance of about eight miles, to spend the day exploring the caves, streams and canyons.

My best friend, Jessie, and I decided our lives would never be complete until we had made a full and complete search of the big ditch. Since we knew very well that our parents would never approve the adventure, we spent a lot of time constructing a story which would enable us to get out of town. Finally we settled on a fairly simple lie of omission and informed our mothers that we were going on a bike trip and would undoubtedly be home by suppertime. We neglected to state our exact destination.

Since Jessie and I were greatly given to the consumption of food, her mother provided us with a wonderful lunch, quite enough for several small girls.

This dear lady, Miss Anna, was a product of the Deep South, and a finer gentlewoman never lived, nor a better cook. She loved to provide after school snacks for us, and one of the great fears of her life was that a visitor would starve to death ere she could get food in front of them. Miss Anna introduced me to the glory of ambrosia, the paradise of fresh coconut cake, and other gastronomical delights too numerous to mention. (Perhaps my life-long struggle with weight control is partially attributable to eating so often at her table, but it was worth every pound of it!)

Jessie's parents were exceptionally kind to me, and I was invited to accompany them on several trips to the "outside" world. My very first overnight stay at a hotel was with them on a visit to the Cotton Carnival. The Peabody Hotel caused one small hill child to open her eyes in wonder. I have ever loved Miss Anna and Mr. Jess for the generosity they seemed happy to show me.

When the big day finally arrived, we armed ourselves with ropes, flashlights and the gargantuan lunch and took off. Following alongside our bicycles was dear old Bow-Wow, beloved canine accomplice of our many childhood escapades. Jessie was an only child (Dear God! how I envied her that blissful state!), and her large, long-haired dog of indeterminate origin was considered by her family to be one of them. (Bow-Wow began sleeping at the foot of Jessie's bed when she entered first grade, and he took his final nap there while she was away at college.)

How that day stands out in my memory. The trek was long, the day was hot, and the houses were few as we progressed into the country. Bow-Wow was our big concern because, being a rather pampered dog, he was rapidly wearing out. We tried taking turns carrying him in our bicycle baskets, but that was not feasible. He was bigger than the bicycles, so our only alternative was to take frequent rest stops.

We requested water for him from several farm wives, who looked askance at us while they inquired (all too frequently) if our parents had any idea at all where we were. Lying heartily, we assured them that half of the town was aware of our whereabouts. They continued to view us with concern. (Not long into the trip we started using false names. We had heard of outlaws doing this and it seemed to add an adventurous and romantic touch to the day.)

When we finally reached our destination, tired, hungry, but still excited, we unpacked our lunch and ate until we were almost blind, a tradition with Jessie and me.

Then we started our conquest of the Gulf! Tying our ropes to the trees lining the canyon, we rappelled down with Bow-Wow and an unknown number of poisonous snakes close at hand. (I wouldn't do such a thing now for ten thousand dollars.)

Such a day! We explored caves which are no longer there due to passage of time and rock slides. We were absolutely positive no one had ever penetrated the caverns to the extreme depths we achieved. Conquerors of Mt. Everest could not have known a greater sense of achievement than did we when we returned home, way after sundown, to face several troubling questions as to just where we had spent the day. Somehow we made it through the inquisition without divulging all the truth.

Years later Jessie and I confessed to her mother about our expedition, and even after the long interval Miss Anna almost had a stroke. Consider her reaction had she known the truth when we were ten years old.

Recently my husband and I took our grandchildren to Grand Gulf State Park, which has been greatly improved upon for the benefit of the many visitors who come to admire the spectacular region. Four overlooks provide imposing views of the gulf, and a long footpath around the chasm, along with stairsteps in the really hilly parts, make the park very accessible.

It had been raining the day we were there, and the trails were a bit slick. The kids started off with grandpa's stern admonitions ringing in their ears; "Be careful now! You might slip and fall. Don't go there, it could be dangerous. Watch out, you're getting too close to the edge. Good Lord, neither one of you can be trusted to do anything! Let's get out of here, Martha, before these kids get killed!"

Smiling through a few tears as I listened to him rant and rave, in my mind's eye I saw two little chubby girls, long brown braids swinging, desperately clinging to ropes and screaming like Tarzan, with a big, completely worn-out dog riding shotgun for them.

Chapter 22

DADDY WAS A DEMOCRAT
AND MAMA CROCHETED

Knocking his chair over as he jumped up from the supper table, Daddy screamed, "Well, God help me but this is just too much!" The little pulse which beat in the left side of his temple when he got upset started jumping with remarkable rapidity. He continued his ranting with "You're just gonna have to unravel the damned thing!!" and the smaller kids left the room because they knew the worst was yet to come. (Also, they had finished eating. You couldn't have run them off with a gun had they still been hungry.)

The evening meal had started off well enough. Anne's fiance', Joe, was eating with us, a not unusual occurrence since he lived with his older sister who could not boil water without burning it. Unless he was knocked away from the table and held back, Joe dined with us almost every night.

Daddy's fit was provoked by an innocent remark from Mama concerning her latest crocheting project, and this seemed odd because he was certainly proud of her expertise in the field.

Most women during the thirties were really into crafts. Some of the work, such as the beautiful quilts which were pieced on summer evenings and quilted during the long, cold, winter nights, was due to necessity, but lots of the ladies had a specialty which was done purely for fun and maybe, just a little, to show off their talents to the world.

Mama's thing was crocheting. She was and is a master of the art, though her eyesight is failing and she can no longer create the beautiful doilies, door panels, and wall hangings she once could. She didn't follow a written pattern, saying she couldn't stand to have a piece of paper tell her what to do, but she could look at any given piece of work and rip it out in record time.

Mama's grandmother taught her the craft when she was a small child. Hanging over my desk is a framed display of some of the work of this dear lady, Granma Bryan. Granma not only created the small doily on display but first picked the cotton, then spun it into thread on her spinning wheel, and finally crocheted the little piece of lace. (This is difficult for me to believe but Mama vows it is true.)

My youngest sister, Leah, seems to be the only one of the family to have inherited a talent for the art. Like Mama, Leah can make almost anything in the world with a crochet hook and a ball of thread.

Since her early childhood the work has fascinated Leah. Once when she was playing with a crochet hook, in some bizarre way it became embedded in her wrist. Crochet hooks are shaped somewhat like fish hooks, and it was difficult to extract, but she managed the removal process without calling for help from Mama. In all probability, seeing Leah with a hook protruding from her wrist would not have done Mama a bit of good.

106

I have told my sister (somewhat bitterly, I'm afraid, since my limited ability in crocheting runs to pot holders and string rugs and I'm not terribly proud of them), that she could crochet a Lincoln Continental if she put her mind to it.

During World War II most folks in town who had a son in the military displayed a star in their window as an indication of the family's contribution to the war effort. Mama found a pattern of a service star which she liked and made one for everyone she knew who qualified for the honor.

The Lord's Prayer was another of her favorites. No telling how many of those she produced over the years.

When my sister, Anne, decided to get married Mama ambitiously undertook to produce the Constitution of the United States of America in ecru crochet for her to hang over the fireplace in her new home. It was her guileless announcement of the new project which caused Daddy to explode with rage. He knew that Joe, the intended husband, was a Republican, and Daddy felt strongly that no one affiliated with the GOP was worthy of displaying the U.S. Constitution in their home in any manner whatsoever, forget about Mama's lovely ecru crochet work.

Daddy was a Democrat. So was almost everyone else in our area. The county "went Republican" only once in recorded history, and Daddy always maintained it happened solely because all the decent folks were down with the flu, and the !@#$% Republicans took unfair advantage of the epidemic. (On the rare occasions when I vote Republican, it would not surprise me for the clouds to part and a tormented voice demand to know just when I had taken leave of my senses! It has not happened yet but I remain uneasy.)

Now Mama was well into Article Three when she made

mention of her intended gift, and Daddy made his announcement that she had just wasted her time. (The entire neighborhood heard the communique.) Mama wept and wailed, but he did not relent so much as to permit her to do the Bill of Rights, and Anne had to settle for a bedspread made of yellow carpet warp. She still has it. Mama's work lasts a long time.

Daddy remained a Democrat until his death, and Joe is still a staunch Republican. As you might envision, we had some fairly heated dialogues around the supper table.

Chapter 23

TEXAS HORSE TRADE

Mama Cash was a "widder woman," and I spent a lot of nights in her home keeping her company and sleeping at the foot of her bed. She entertained me with many interesting stories of by-gone years, and my favorite topic was the trip her family had made to Texas in a covered wagon.

Her father, like so many other young men following the Civil War, was given to moving around a good bit, and when he heard of the great things going on in the Lone Star State he just packed up his large family and took off. Six girls and one boy made the trip. According to Mama Cash, that little boy was spoiled so bad salt couldn't save him.

The story always started with "Oh, how that Texas wind did blow! Maw couldn't get any cookin' done before dust and dirt covered everything." Mama Cash hated any sort of untidiness and the fact that they didn't take a bath or wash their hair for nearly a month caused her to blush with embarrassment when she related the story to me some fifty years after the event.

The travelers had a run-in one day with what she described as "a sorry lookin' bunch of Indians" who wanted to make a horse trade of sorts. (Mama Cash did not see the native Americans as romantic. The ones she encountered on the trip were dirty and she could not abide dirt.) Her family was traveling alone, which doesn't say a lot concerning the common sense of my great-grandpa, and they became more than a little upset when the Indians came upon them.

One of the girls, Rosella, was riding a pretty, young mare which was gentle and extremely attractive, as was Rosella. The head honcho of the Indians, through grunts and sign language, indicated his desire to make some sort of trade. Nothing satisfactory was ever worked out, because after a lot of palavering it was determined that the young Indian wanted Rosella and not her mare!

Mama Cash always laughed at this point of the story and remarked she thought her dad should have made the trade, since another horse would have been a lot more useful on the trip than Rosella turned out to be. (Rosella was not her favorite sister.)

The family stayed in Texas less than two years, hardly time to get everyone clean and the quilts washed to hear my grandmother tell it.

They talked her dad into making the return trip to Missouri by train which was much more enjoyable than the covered wagon.

You couldn't get Mama Cash to go on a camping trip if your life depended on it. She wasn't even real big on picnics.

Chapter 24

SONGS AND SAGAS OF THE ROCKING CHAIR

Lots of times after supper, especially in the long winter months when Daddy would be out on his fox hunting excursions, Mama would entertain us by playing our old upright piano (which weighed seventeen tons) and singing dreary, sorrowful ballads about sudden death, destruction, and public execution. Mama did not read music, but she could "chord" and we certainly didn't know the difference. The old songs were dear to us.

You may not be familiar with this one, called by the brief and catchy title of "Georgie's Mother Ran to Him With a Basket on Her Arm."

> Georgie's mother ran to him with a basket on her arm.
> She said, "My darling son, be careful how you run.
> For many poor boys have lost their lives, just trying to gain lost time,
> And if you run your engine right, you'll get there just on time."

(Even as sons today, he obviously paid no attention to her because...)

> Up the track he darted and against the rock he crashed.
> Upside down the engine turned and George was bent and smashed.
> His head against the firebox door, the flames a-rollin' high.
> He said, "I'm glad I was born an engineer, on my final run to die."
>
> The doctor came to Georgie, he said, "Oh George, lie still!
> Your life may yet be saved, if it is God's holy will."
> George said, "Oh, no, I want to die...I want to die so free.
> I want to die by the side of the engine I love, old Hundred and Ninety-three."

(Does that statement seem odd to you? I have never been able to figure it out.)

> The doctor said to Georgie, "Your life cannot be saved.
> You were murdered on the railroad, you'll lie in a lonesome grave."
> His face was covered up with blood, his eyes you could not see,
> And the very last words poor Georgie said were, "Near my God to Thee!"

> —author unknown—

Don't those words just make you feel good all over?

You may have picked up that this is a song about railroading. My family was (and is) deeply involved in "workin' on the road," and lots of the songs we especially enjoyed pertained to frightful train wrecks with bodies lying strewn along the tracks.

In my mind's eye as I listened to Mama singing of the

horrible and destructive tragedies, I could see folks running from far and near to get close to the injured. Taking notes, they would record the dying utterances of the victims, I thought, so as to later write songs about the catastrophe, lest posterity forget the event. We were devoted to the old ballads, and oddly enough we never worried about any of our relatives getting hurt in a train wreck.

Mama didn't sing "Casey Jones." It wasn't grisly enough to appeal to us.

While lulling the baby of the family to sleep in a squeaking old rocker, she would sing mournful, sad, tear-evoking lullabies which hang in my memory even today.

(For some reason I used to like to stick my foot under the rocker if I had on shoes, and that would drive Mama crazy. She would slap my face if I was within easy reach. I've heard any number of people say they had the same obsession as a child, and I've never been able to figure out the fascination.)

Anyway, my all-time favorite lullaby-type song was about some runaways who got lost and ended up dead. I never lost any sleep over them, figuring they got what they deserved and even used it to sing my daughter to sleep, hoping it would serve to keep her near home.

The unforgettable words follow: (They alone are worth the price of this book!)

Oh, don't you remember a long time ago.
There were two little babies their names I don't know.
Went strolling away, one bright summer day,
Got lost in the woods, I've heard people say.

And when it was night, so sad was their plight.
The moon went down and the stars gave no light.
They sobbed and they sighed, they bitterly cried,
Those two little babies, they lay down and died.

113

And when they were dead the birdies so red,
Brought strawberry leaves and over them spread.
So sing me a song the whole night long,
Of babies in the woods, little babies in the woods.
—author unknown—

I'm not sure of the name of that little jewel, but several years ago I overheard my granddaughter crying and saying, "Please Mama, rock me and sing 'Don' cha' 'member'...Please, please, sing 'Don' cha' 'member'..."

I guess it's true that really great music never dies. I know that song has gone through at least four generations.

When she got tired of singing, Mama would switch over to stories of her younger days. Those tales of the past, many of them quite strange, were as fascinating to us as were the songs.

The oddest one I can recall concerns the time the community buried Joe Morris and he came back to give personal testimony to the mistake. As I remember, Mama's version went like this.

Joe and Clara, along with their three small children, lived in the Oak Grove community where Mama and Daddy resided early in their married life, the late twenties. The tiny, scrubby, hill farms peculiar to this locale could not provide much in the way of livelihood, to say nothing of any measure of comfort, and most of the family men would periodically leave for a more prosperous area, work for a time and return home for the winter months or for so long as their slim savings would allow. So it was with Joe.

During one of his absences Clara did not hear from him for a long time and this was unusual, since he was a good family man and deeply concerned for his children.

Imagine the shock and consternation which swept over the neighborhood when word was received by the Morris family that Joe had been involved in a grocery store robbery out in Kansas. When he tried to flee the scene, he was shot and killed by a local police officer.

Knowing Joe as they did, folks found this news hard to swallow, especially his mother, who was a "shouting Methodist."

Perhaps I should clarify this branch of Methodism. In the early twentieth century, we Methodists were known for joyful, prolonged singing unto the Lord, and interspersed with this worship was an occasional, spontaneous outburst of enthusiastic "shouting" which was looked on by everyone not blood related to the shouter with amused but loving tolerance. (We have now come a long way from this in our church, being at the present time about as spontaneous as milk going bad in the hot sun. This should in no way be construed as boasting.)

Anyway, the family recovered the body, final arrangements were completed for the service, and plans were made for the family to stay at our home the night before and after the funeral.

Several people commented after the service that being shot at, hit, and killed had really changed old Joe's looks. Daddy, ever tactful, chose an opportune moment to casually mention to Clara that mistakes could happen in situations such as this, and for her to remember that Joe just might show up sometime in the future.

That's exactly what happened! In he walked a couple of months after the big funeral, and the mistake was never fully explained.

Joe lived to a ripe old age and was the only man around who could say with the immortal Mark Twain, "The report of my death has been greatly exaggerated."

The funniest story in her stock was about one of our uncles who didn't get what he wanted for Christmas. His reaction to the intense disppointment was singular, to say

115

the least.

When the requested pony failed to show up under the Christmas tree, Uncle Web's frustration knew no bounds. In order to show his unhappiness, he decided to withdraw from the world and hide behind the living room door.

Uncle Web was an easily bored child and since there wasn't a lot to do for amusement behind the portal after he brushed away the cobwebs and dusted off the wood-work, the little boy undertook to stretch his mouth around the doorknob. This turned into quite a project since the knob was not one of the little, shiny things we have now but rather was quite large and brass, with lots of ornate carvings.

After considerable effort, Uncle was successful beyond his wildest dreams and got the entire doorknob into his mouth. Unhappily he was not equally successful when he tried to remove his mouth from around the same doorknob.

As you might guess, before long his mother heard muted sounds of distress coming from behind the door; muted, of course, because he couldn't scream really loud since the doorknob acted as a sort of brass gag.

All attempts by the family to help the small child in the removal process were to no avail. Eventually they had to take the door off the hinges, put Uncle Web on top of it and carry both child and door seven miles in a flat-bed wagon to reach a doctor. The alcoholic, fat, medical man laughed so hard at the unusual spectacle that he fell to the floor, as in a fit.

After a significant length of time they were able to revive the M.D., who removed the knob surgically from Uncle Web's mouth.

None of us kids ever gave any thought at all of trying to stretch our mouths around a doorknob. We had seen Uncle Web.

Chapter 25

YOU SCREAM! I SCREAM!
WE ALL SCREAM FOR ICE CREAM!

The old man violently flung the dish of ice cream at the dog, grabbed his head with both hands and shrieked, "My God! My God!" at the top of his voice. Following the scream, he dropped to his hands and knees to slowly crawl through the crowd, earnestly and prayerfully imploring God to save him from his folly. Such a performance really caught the attention of the small group assembled in our back yard, who agreed it was a most unusual way to start an ice cream party.

Several neighbors had been invited in that afternoon to share in the simple pleasure of making ice cream in an old rusty freezer. Back in the hills, when we were growing up, it was rare for the family to eat a whole batch without guests to share the enjoyment. Almost always someone called in a few friends, and they would bring a contribution in the form of a chocolate cake or possibly a fresh peach cobbler. Sometimes the event grew into an eating orgy of monumental proportions, and I always ap-

117

proved of that.

One of the visitors on this warm July afternoon was an elderly gentleman who had accepted our invitation after working for a long while in his garden. Being extremely hot and tired from his labor, he was the first in line when we started serving, and without any formality at all he started shoveling the ice cream into his heat-exhausted body.

Now if you have ever eaten much ice cream, homemade or otherwise, you will undoubtedly recognize this to be the wrong thing for him to do. It didn't take him very long to realize it, either, and quickly his look of pleasure and delight turned to one of complete and total agony. Most of us knew gut level what he was experiencing, but we had never before seen anyone react to the pain as he did.

Slowly he crawled through the little assembly, carefully weaving his way through the straight-backed kitchen chairs and their occupants. (Lawn furniture was an unknown in those days. We just carried the kitchen chairs out to the back yard for our get-togethers.) Occasionally the old fellow lifted his head high in the air and intensified his divine supplications. (Anne said later that his performance reminded her a lot of one of the hounds baying when the moon was full.)

All of us kids wanted to laugh so bad our eyes almost popped out of our heads, but we stifled the desire, knowing full well that Mama or Daddy would surely beat us to death with the BELT if we so much as grinned. (In those days small children did not laugh at adults no matter how great the desire.)

The elderly man slowly circled the yard, stopping occasionally to paw in the grass like a horse with a bad case of colic. After a considerable time his screams diminished to moans, then sobs, and finally he was able to get to his feet, helped by one of the sympathetic viewers who had been watching the therapeutic crawl with great interest. Indeed, it was something to see.

When he was sufficiently recovered our friend quietly returned to his gardening work. I was told he declined a second helping of ice cream. (It baffled me that anyone could decline a second helping of ice cream!) Later he was heard to remark that after our little gathering he just lost all desire for cold foodstuffs.

Our clan seemed rather given to incidents of this nature. Another occurrence, which could have been extremely serious, took place on a hot afternoon during the preparations for creating a gallon of my favorite dessert.

My little brothers, Bert and Reg, were taking turns slapping a gunny sack full of ice with the flat side of an ax blade. It had to be done (in case you are young and feel this to be a somewhat unusual occupation) to reduce a large block of ice into small chips. The little pieces could then be easily packed around the metal container which held the ingredients necessary to produce the final delightful product. (Remember, we are talking about a time of long ago when crushed ice was not available on every street corner.)

Bert, being almost two years the elder, felt he should give his little brother a few pointers on the art of wielding the ax. Reg, feeling fairly confident of his ability to crush ice, declined all instruction and refused to turn over the tool. He was having a lot of fun and was not greatly given to sharing, anyway. (For example, when Daddy would bring us stale cinnamon rolls from the store, Reg always refused to share with anyone. If he was not given a whole package for himself, he wouldn't eat a bite!)

In order to emphasize his determination to take over the ice crushing task, Bert (very unwisely as it turned out)

119

placed his bare foot on the sack of ice chips, daring Reg (so to speak) to do anything about it. That action proved to be very imprudent on his part.

Reg, never a talkative or argumentative child as were the rest of us, quite simply raised the ax which he had been using in such a helpful way and tried his level best to cut his brother's big toe off! Though not totally successful, he came pretty close to realizing his objective. But his aim was either a bit faulty or the toe was tougher than he had estimated when he made his swing, because the digit was left dangling to the foot by a large shred of skin.

Well, as you might guess, the ensuing cries of both Bert and myself brought Mama rushing to the scene. Crying copiously, as was her habit when any of us sustained these accidents so common to big families, she got a can of Red Hollyhock Salve from our almost limitless supply. Smearing the greasy stuff generously on the semi-amputation, she tied his toe back onto his foot with a strip of torn up pillow case. (We saved all the old, worn-out bed linens for just such emergencies. They came in handy from time to time.)

Luckily, Daddy was not at home to become involved in this mess, and we had to do without the services of the Great God Almighty, who was normally called into action at times of family crisis. (We kids were not allowed to plead for help from our Heavenly Father in the same manner as did Daddy. He had informed us on numerous occasions that just because he was on a first name basis with the Lord, it did not necessarily follow that any and all idiots of his production could follow suit! Daddy explained things very carefully.)

Now old Bert was tough, and the toe healed with no bad side effects except for being black as coal, with little or no feeling. (This proved to be helpful later in his high school

120

football career. He broke that toe several times and didn't even know it.)

After grafting the toe back on, we finished making the ice cream. Bert got to eat his brother's share because, after thinking over the episode, Reggie was really sorry about the whole thing. He ran off and hid in the woods and didn't even make it home by suppertime.

Chapter 26

MAMA CASH, PIONEER

For the most part pioneer hill women were a sturdy breed. They had no choice in the matter, for only the strong could survive the problems life inflicted upon them on an almost daily basis.

My paternal grandmother, Mama Cash, could serve as a prototype of the age. Widowed early in life, she was left with seven sons and a daughter to bring up by herself. In his youth, during the Spanish-American War, my grandfather served in the army and he died at an early age of a service-related injury. No doubt the pension my grandmother received from the military was woefully inadequate to maintain any type of livelihood for the large family other than basic survival.

Several of her boys dropped out of school, as did many other young people of that era, and they earned what they could to help. Mama Cash was an excellent seamstress and did lots of tailoring for the more affluent ladies of the town. (I've been the proud possessor of a few of her pretty

123

creations which were sewn on the pedal-type sewing machine she used for much of her life.) The family grew a huge garden, canned everything they didn't eat, kept a cow and chickens, but even with all that, there was not a lot left for extras.

During World War I, as well as World War II, school children were encouraged to buy government saving stamps, and the purchases were made during the first class of the day. These stamps would be stuck in a little cardboard folder, and when enough were accumulated, a trade could be made for a war bond. Now the Cash kids did not have any money to invest in the military effort, being hard put to get enough to eat, and some of their classmates noticed the fact.

These fellow students took it upon themselves to indulge in a bit of ridicule and name-calling, somehow feeling justified in labeling all those who could not buy the stamps as endorsing the German ruler of the time, Kaiser Wilhelm II. (Remember hearing about him in school?) At every opportune moment the youthful harassers would yell "KAISER BILL" at the kids who could not afford to buy the stamps, and the Cash boys, among the others, endured the taunts in silent, red-faced embarrassment.

The boys said nothing to their mother of the situation, knowing that she had her hands full with other problems, but eventually their reluctance to attend school on stamp purchasing day became obvious. My grandmother demanded to know the reason, and the boys finally told her.

The youngsters had underestimated their mother's ability to handle such a situation. Tightening her lips, as was her habit when upset, she marched off to school next day with her boys in hand.

One by one each boy's classroom was visited and the teachers, after one glance at the frosty-eyed caller, gladly gave her all the time she needed to talk with the scholars. The children looked on with wide-eyed interest as this unusual lady explained just why her children were unable to support the war effort at this point in their lives. In a firm, steady voice she informed them that her sons had given to their country not dimes, but their dad and not one of the tormentors could claim a greater contribution.

I have been told by people who were in her audience that day that few eyes were dry at the end of her impressive speech, and the name-calling was finished.

Like most young kids, her boys loved to swim and, since pools were unknown in those days, they utilized the small creek which ran through town. (As a matter of fact, Warm Fork was still used as the local cooling-off place when I was growing up.) A large cottonwood tree grew close to the bank of the little stream, and the swimmers used it for diving purposes, climbing as high as they dared before jumping into the deepest part of the water.

One summer was much dryer than normal, and my Uncle Mel mistook the depth of the water, hit the bottom, and encountered a big, sharp rock in the process. As you might guess, the result was a nasty gash in his head. One of the locals, feeling sympathy for his plight, picked him up in a wagon and carried him to his back door. As with most head wounds, his was bleeding profusely.

Mama Cash was one of the most meticulous house-keepers who ever lived, even though she was bringing up a herd of boys, and she certainly did not allow bleeding on the interior premises if it could possibly be avoided. When Uncle Mel attempted to enter the house, she pushed him out the back door, yelled at my Aunt Lorena (who had the unhappy fate of being the only girl in the family) to bring out the haircutting equipment and the fur started to fly! Using clippers, razors, and other necessary tools, Mama

Cash shaved her son's head and plastered the gaping wound together with what served in those days as adhesive tape.

That hot summer day my uncle acquired, along with the big hole in his head, a life-long nickname of "Baldy."

One of her sons made the tragic mistake one morning of trying to "hop a freight" instead of going to school. The result was a terrible accident in which the young man lost a leg. After his long hospital stay (even Mama Cash saw the need for outside help with a problem of this magnitude), this high school basketball star began his long trek from home back to class on crutches.

News of his return preceded him, and he had barely begun his journey when he was met by most of the student body, hoisted onto willing shoulders and escorted back to school to continue his interrupted education.

Ironically, his class had been studying the classics, and the character of Long John Silver, the peg-leg pirate of *Treasure Island* fame, was fresh in their minds. The class clown had a wonderful idea, and until the day he died, my uncle answered to the name of "John" more frequently than to his given name.

On a squirrel hunting expedition one day, another of Mama Cash's boys somehow managed to shoot off a thumb and a fair amount of his index finger. He was alone in the woods and almost bled to death before reaching medical help. The doctor had no means of giving a blood transfusion and only provided basic first aid to the child, saying, "Get him to his mother as fast as you can. He can't live!"

The doctor underestimated the medical skills of Mama Cash and the stubborn streak for survival which runs in our family. The funeral was held sixty years later. For some reason, my uncle didn't acquire a nickname from his accident. Perhaps it was felt such a close brush with eternity should not be trivialized in any way.

When telling such stories, Mama Cash would often say, "If they all made it home by suppertime in one piece, I considered it a pretty good day."

Chapter 27

SHOOT ME, FOR GOD'S SAKE!
JUST SHOOT ME!

For some reason our clan had an overwhelming, almost psychopathic fear of anything remotely related to the dental profession. Any one of us would break out in a cold sweat whenever a dull ache or pain in the area of the jaw told us we were in for a visit to our personal chamber of horrors, the office of Dr. Hillis, our dentist and one of Daddy's good hunting friends.

You have to remember, back in those days kids were not taken to the dentist unless there was a serious problem, usually necessitating the removal of a tooth. (You can forget about your six month checkups.) Well do I remember passing out flat, stone cold on the dental office floor, not from pain, mind you, but from sheer terror of the unknown, and I was eighteen years old! First time in my life to be in a dentist's office.

I've never completely recovered from the agony of anxiety, but time has somewhat mellowed my stress. Still, the only thing I remotely enjoy about a shot of novacaine is being able to imitate Buddy Hackett.

My earliest recollection of mandibular problems dates way back to a summer visit with my grandparents. Their farm was so isolated and removed from medical and/or dental services that Good Papa was on rare occasions pressed into practice as an apprentice dentist. He had a few basic, old-fashioned instruments with which to ply his unhappy trade, and I'm afraid extracting forceps lay high on his list of working utensils.

One day a young lady who was suffering greatly from toothache was brought to the farm by her parents. The poor thing was pleading to be put out of her misery with a bullet right between the eyes, or for some merciful soul to hit her on the head with one of the large pieces of iron ore which covered the ground around the barn. (The area serving as Good Papa's dental office was right beside the old log corn crib.) Her big mistake of the day came when she opened her mouth, as requested by Good Papa, and the next few minutes were indescribable. Just believe me, it was bad and gave me material for nightmares for years to come.

To say that we were all cowards concerning dental problems would be the understatement of the year, yet Mama swore we older ones were heroic giants of unlimited courage when compared with the baby of the family, Larry. When work was needed on his teeth, he started screaming well before leaving home, and didn't stop for several days following the event. Needless to say, the dentist did not look forward to visits from my youngest brother. I'm sure if Dr. Hillis and Daddy hadn't been such close friends, Larry would have been refused an appointment.

He has recently handled the denture problem well, though. Entering the hospital, Larry demanded and received general anesthesia for the extracting work, and lay for several days in the Intensive Care Unit. (Several of the staff thought him to be dying, when the screams from his room of "Shoot me!! For God's sake, just shoot me!" would shatter the midnight hours.

Speedy and I realized when our daughter's baby teeth started loosening that she unluckily had inherited my familial weakness. After noticing some of her classmates with glaringly obvious gaps in their mouths, even promises of a visit from the Tooth Fairy would not induce her to let anyone check the condition of her mouth. (Lea had overheard conversations at school about "pullin' teeth" and she wanted no part of it.)

One early evening while she was taking her bath Speedy (having planned his strategy well in advance), casually remarked, "Lea, open your mouth and let old Dad see if you have any loose teeth." (He thought he was playing it cool with the "old Dad" bit, but it didn't work.)

In a lot less time than it takes to tell, the child jumped out of the tub, slithered past the both of us (being totally uncatchable covered as she was with soap) and made for the safety of the woods! (We lived on a small farm at the time and had no close neighbors to witness Lea's origination of the "streaker" phenomenon.) She covered a lot of territory for a barefooted, nude child in a blackberry patch, I have to tell you.

That scene would have tickled a dog, and I just collapsed on the ground. My husband, always a more dutiful parent than I, tried to lure her home by bellowing into the darkening woods that he'd buy her a Shetland pony if she would come on back. It was good dark before she reappeared.

Something has happened to water down this hereditary fear because I frequently take Lea's children to the dentist and orthodontist (who, incidentally, has got to be one of the wealthiest men in Mississippi, possibly the U. S. of A.) and they don't even require handcuffs.

Chapter 28

IN DEFENSE OF THE
MATHEMATICALLY INCAPACITATED

Entering school wasn't easy for my youngest sister, Leah, one of the last of our clan to make that big step into adulthood. The teachers having been cursed by the Cash progeny who came before her knew just about what to expect and judiciously kept an eye peeled in her direction from kindergarten through high school.

It wasn't that the Cash kids were what you could call mean or dumb students; we just weren't good or smart. Rather in the median range and that was what we wanted! No midnight study for us, yet we managed to be in the top half of our respective classes and could devote most of our time to entertaining friends and driving educators berserk. We felt such activity to be much more laudable and rewarding than making good grades or gaining information. Like students of today, we were serene in the knowledge that all wisdom was ours, and school was for us just a light-hearted social event, certainly not to be taken seriously.

133

Probably the only real weakness so far as intelligence was concerned in our household was that every one of us suffered severe difficulties when dealing with higher mathematics. Simple stuff we got readily. No problem with the basics such as fractions, percentages, balance the check book, etc. But just throw in some geometry, trigonometry, even algebra, and we all had to run for cover. To use a modern day expression, we just did not compute.

Leah was aware of this flaw in our genetic pool and why she ever enrolled in algebra is a mystery to me. Perhaps it was required. Perhaps the registrar did not recognize her name as being one of the afflicted. Perhaps they were all drunk. I don't know. But I do know that after the third day the class had gone way beyond her feeble sphere of ability to assimilate mathematical information. Following family tradition, she quite naturally turned her talents to causing trouble and grief for the teacher, Mr. Parven Miller.

This fine man, totally devoted to imparting knowledge to recalcitrant scholars, had in prior years put up with four Cash kids so when my sister walked into his class he knew what to expect and was more than ready.

Leah's best friend, Lois, was taking the class and tried hard to grasp the algebraic concepts being thrown her way. Being a conscientious student, she desperately sought to get her daily work in on time. Leah, knowing full well she was going to flunk out of the class before the month was over, made no attempt to keep abreast of the assignments. Totally content, she expended her time and energy in teasing and tormenting those unfortunates who sat around her. Lois was seated on my sister's "right hand" (scripturally speaking), and thus suffered the full force of her fun-loving ways.

A small problem developed when Lois, a "neat freak," wore the erasers off her pencils almost before the lead was sharpened. She began to get on my sister's nerves with her frequent requests to borrow an eraser so Leah, ever a resourceful child, devised a devilish scheme to break her friend of the habit.

Early in her high school career, Leah had made the uncommon discovery that by cutting off the head of a straight pen she could push the remainder down into a pencil eraser. She could leave a tiny bit sticking out, not enough for anyone to see but ample to completely shred a paper should anyone be foolish enough to use it for purposes of correction.

Leah's evil plan involved the use of this instrument of destruction.

Class had just started when Lois (a model of deportment) very quietly requested the use of Leah's pencil eraser. Just as quietly, Leah gave it to her. As the totally neat algebra paper was reduced to little more than confetti, thrills of joy shot through my sister's body. Lois, not given to handling stress well at all, burst into wracking sobs which of course caught the attention of Mr. Miller, their long-suffering teacher.

A brief inspection of the riddled remains of the algebra paper apprised him of Leah's sin. She was invited to step into the hall where the pent-up passion of years of dealing with Cash kids finally was released upon her hapless (though certainly not innocent) head.

She was informed in no uncertain terms that Mr. Miller had (using a direct quote) "taken it" from four of her siblings (starting with me) and he did not intend, "God help him!" to "take it" from another Cash idiot! As God was his witness, he shrieked, he would quit his job first! (Mr. Miller must have been totally unnerved because I

135

think he had some small children at that time, and he was not a wealthy man. I'm sure he needed to work.)

Leah was greatly shocked for Mr. Miller was known to be a calm sort and not greatly given to wild fits of rage. My sister tried to explain that she meant no harm, but he told her, almost screaming, that he knew better and for her to shut her face and listen to him. (At this point little flecks of spittle started to collect in the corners of his mouth and a tiny pulse was jumping violently in his left temple.) As he continued the tirade, Leah grew fearful that he might have a stroke, and she wondered how she could ever explain the situation should anything catastrophic occur.

Mr. Miller seemed to remember a lot about the whole family, and he took morbid delight in dredging up every past sin any of us had ever committed in his class. It took him some time to vividly paint his disagreeable picture of the Cash clan, and he was panting and slavering more than a little by the time he reached the grand finale. All in all it was just an ugly scene, Leah said.

He refused to allow her to explain her side of the story. Hoping to evoke a little sympathy, she mentioned our familial weakness in the area of mathematics but he didn't swallow it. By this time his voice had weakened considerably, and he could only huskily mouth that we were in no way mathematically incapacitated but simply as lazy as a bunch of hound dogs, and he stated further that he would rather die than see another one of us walk into his classroom.

Daddy resented the remark about the hound dogs. He didn't deny it. He just resented it.

EMERGENCY
ROOM
⟶

Chapter 29

KEROSINE CAN OR EMERGENCY ROOM?

Ours was not the only family that took childhood injuries rather lightly. My friend Dorothy had a close brush with a do-it-yourself attempt at decapitation which resulted in a broken vertebra and not one of her relatives seemed unduly concerned at the time. Dorothy's story seems somewhat incredulous when compared with present day health practices.

Some fifty years ago it was her brother David's practice to ride the family horse to town for their weekly supply of absolute necessities. We are not talking here about frivolous items such as canned vegetables, bread, milk, eggs, etc. but rather flour, sugar, coffee, cornmeal, salt, and baking powder. Such were the items which constituted essentials in those days, not the diet soda, chocolate chip cookies, potato chips and hair conditioner which head the list of indispensable needs today.

Almost always when David returned home Dorothy would be permitted to ride Old Charlie for a few minutes, just around the yard, with her brother leading the horse. (She was the only girl in the family and they didn't want to lose her.) But for some reason on this particular day he did not see fit to follow his habit and refused to take the time to let her enjoy her favorite activity.

Being stubborn to a fault (her own words), she determined to ride the animal anyway and somehow managed to climb onto his back when no one was looking, without the usual help given by her brother. She encountered a small problem when she looked over her shoulder to see if anyone was attempting to stop her. The horse sped up and took her directly under the wire clothesline, which practically cut her head off, and caused her to become unsettled, unseated, and flung violently to the ground.

She knew herself to be hurt. Dorothy was an astute child and realized that in all probability the human body could not undergo such an experience without sustaining problems of a serious nature. Still, she resisted complaining very much because she knew her brother would (in all probability) say "It's all your own fault!" or maybe "Why don't you ever listen to a word you're told?" and in her mangled state she did not welcome such remarks.

With the peeled back and rolled up skin of her neck smarting more than a little, and her pounding head giving distinct testimony to the rock she had encountered in the fall, Dorothy undertook to render unto herself first aid. She located an old piece of tea towel and having heard somewhere that kerosine had healing qualities, she gave the makeshift bandage a good soaking in the miracle liquid before tying it loosely around her injured neck.

She lived. Her neck was black and blue for weeks but she lived.

Years later when age necessitated X rays being made of her spinal area a young doctor casually asked how she had received her broken neck. Searching her memory, Dorothy recounted the story to him and he was stunned.

I guess those stories of folks surviving a hanging are true. An untreated broken neck isn't necessarily terminal. Just ask Dorothy.

Let me tell you of another incident concerning a horse-back mishap.

It occurred on the day of our daughter's wedding. The ceremony had gone off without a hitch and it was a lovely affair. Friends and relatives from far and near had honored us by filling the church nearly to capacity.

The reception was held at our place with the large crowd overflowing into the yard. As it began to wind down the out-of-town guests started making their leisurely way to the home of my sister, Iris, to enjoy the lavish buffet supper which she had provided.

After the bridal couple made their escape, I tried politely but without much success to get rid of the hangers-on so Speedy and I could join the others in the eating orgy we knew was taking place.

I feared trouble was about to occur when one of the city visitors strolled casually into the yard leading my husband's young gelding, Sunny, by a rotten binder twine string.

As a general rule, Speedy is quiet, calm, placid, and not at all given to claims of glory for himself, but he does love to show off his equestrian skills. He is a good horseman, no doubt about it.

Quickly he took the rotten string, grasped the mane of the young palomino and effortlessly swung onto the broad, bare back, a feat which I'd give a year off my life to be able to do. In less time than it takes to tell, Sunny was put into a canter, Speedy was looking great, and the watching crowd was murmuring appreciatively, when the string broke. The rider, fearing imminent disaster, loudly yelled, "Whoa!"

Sunny, being the well-trained quarter horse that he was, quickly responded to instructions. He planted all four feet firmly in the ground which naturally caused his occupant to sail through the air and skid briefly over the rocky terrain. As Speedy's head plowed into the drought-stricken August soil, his ear, which protrudes more than somewhat, took the brunt of the fall and the results were ghastly, to say the very least.

The crew on duty in the emergency room of our local hospital, who through the very nature of their work saw lots of odd happenings, was more than a little amazed when they viewed what was left of Speedy's ear. It was not a pretty sight. Hanging loosely by a few thin shreds of skin, it almost reached his shoulder and indeed, was not a pretty sight. One rather articulate intern, in the midst of reattaching Speedy's ear, remarked that the damage reminded him a lot of a partially skinned squirrel. (I guess the young man had hunted a lot before turning to medicine.)

When you compare a peeled ear to a broken neck, you just have to agree there is considerable difference in medical attention then and now.

Speedy went to the emergency room. Dorothy went to the kerosine can.

Chapter 30

YOU CAN TAKE A GIRL
OUT OF THE HILLS BUT...

It has been called to my attention on numerous occasions, and I believe it to be true, that the accent which I acquired while growing up in the hill country has not diminished in the least during my forty or so years of living in a "far country." When I'm visiting in my hometown often someone will tap me on the shoulder and say, "Hi, Martha, I wasn't sure that was you until I heard you speak. I'd know your voice anywhere." It's nice to be remembered, even if only for an appalling accent.

When I entered college in my middle years one of my teachers, a speech therapist, let me know right away that in my case the old saying was true; "You can take a girl out of the hills, but you can't take the hills out of the girl." At least, he said, this was true of my speech. I learned to take the ribbing and kidding but I never learned to enjoy it.

Until I started taking speech classes I never realized that some considered me handicapped by having grown up in

141

the Ozarks. Gut level I always felt most people, given a choice, would want a childhood such as our family had, culturally and materially deprived though we may have been.

One of the education courses we beginning teachers were required to take was called "Oral Interpretation," and it supposedly taught one to read stories to small children. The fact that I had been reading stories to small children for thirty-odd years, with no small success I might add, did not impress the Office of the Registrar.

My teacher, Dr. William Cobb (I'll never forget him, never!), found much to criticize about me when I made my first class presentation. Most of it concerned my Ozark "drawl," as he put it. I was not greatly surprised when he asked me to make myself available for a conference in his office, where the following conversation took place.

"Now, Martha, I want you to seriously consider enrolling in our speech correction program here at the University. I'm afraid your accent is not going to be acceptable in the job market, and you need to work on the problem. I suggest you get yourself signed up right away, the sooner the better."

More than a little offended, I replied, "Well, Dr. Cobb (Those Ph.D. people insist on being called DOCTOR!), I have been able to communicate fairly well for some forty years with no great trouble. I have this accent because I grew up in the Ozark region and..."

"Yes, yes, I know," he interrupted. "I'm aware of your background. It shows up every time you open your mouth, and you need to realize what a handicap it may prove to be." And on and on he continued, making me madder by the moment as he added insult to injury concerning my upbringing. He concluded with, "Why, do you have any idea what we do with hillbillies up here at the university?"

Dripping sarcasm, I replied, "No, Dr. Cobb, I don't know what you do with hillbillies up here at the university, but it can't be much worse than what we do with cobs over in Oregon County."

Guess what I made in that class?

Several years ago a dream came true for me when I was privileged to visit the British Isles with a tour group of alumni from midwestern colleges. We hit all the tourist attractions which included the Changing of the Guards at Buckingham Palace. Standing in back of the fence which was there for the sole purpose of keeping trashy folks like me from getting too close to the Royal Family, in my enthusiasm I was talking a mile a minute.

There was quite a crowd around and at first I thought the tapping on my shoulder was accidental, but it continued until I turned around and was confronted with a very, very English young lady who politely asked, "Would you please tell me if you are from the midwestern United States?" I admitted to the fault and she further inquired, "Could it be southern Missouri?" I again acknowledged the shortcoming. When she finally quizzed, "Am I correct in thinking you could be from the Ozark hill country along the Arkansas and Missouri border?" I could only nod my head.

She explained that her interest stemmed from her study of worldwide speech patterns, and in me she had found a classic, textbook example of the Ozark accent.

I had traveled thousands of miles away from home, but it took only a few seconds for that linguistic student from Oxford to take me back to the hills.

Chapter 31

END OF THE LINE

By the end of their childbearing years, Mama and Daddy had accumulated eight children, four of each gender, and that was a sizeable litter even in those days of big families. Daddy often jokingly remarked (I THINK he was joking), "I don't know why Clair keeps havin' babies, but if it's what I suspect she won't be stoppin' anyways soon." I'm sure they didn't need all of us and probably didn't even want all of us, but there always seemed to be enough love to go around.

Our clan was spaced out over a period of about twenty years so I was grown before the babies of the family were old enough to get into really serious trouble. Most of their growing up escapades are not known to me, but at a Thanksgiving gathering not many years back I heard about one stunt the two youngest members pulled which certainly bears repeating.

Mama was well-known for her ability to create the best corn bread dressing this side of heaven, and after we were grown all of us looked forward to bringing our own families back home for holiday meals. In the finest tradition of the hills we would eat until we fell away from the table.

My youngest sister, Leah, and the baby of the family, Larry, got sick and tired of hearing us brag about this special dish Mama made. They were called into service in small ways, such as chopping onions, celery, etc. and the youngsters deeply resented it. One holiday they decided to put a stop to the idea that Mama was better than the average when it came to making corn bread dressing.

Putting their heads together, they came up with a plan built around fishing worms. It was in no way complicated. In a fertile area of the garden which had loose soil, they went to work with their worm digging equipment and before long they had a bountiful supply of night crawlers. Not even bothering to brush away the dirt which clung to some portions of the earthworms, they cut and mashed the squirming mass into tiny bits or bites, depending on how you view the matter. When Mama wasn't looking, they dropped their gourmet offering into the huge bowl of raw ingredients which would be used in preparing the next day's corn bread dressing.

No one was the wiser since they stirred the mixture well, and the mashed worms looked a lot like chopped sage.

At the big meal they heard several comments concerning the wonderful food, and the general consensus was that Mama had done it again! Best corn bread dressing in the world!

You want to talk about a couple of disappointed kids?

Since the two were the end of the line, lots of small chores fell to them, and many of these jobs lay within the area of the barnyard. Leah and Larry vow it is a wonder they ever made it to adulthood considering the lethal creatures of destruction with which they were forced to contend.

By their report even the cows were dangerous. Both of them swear that somewhere deep within the soul of the bovine species lurks an overwhelming desire to inflict pain and suffering on anyone who approaches them with a milk bucket.

Larry has been overheard to remark bitterly that all the cows he was acquainted with in childhood loved to slap small boys across the eyes with their hairy tails. Since these attachments were usually totally covered in dried manure, the experience was not pleasant to say the least, and was exceedingly hard on the eyes. He suspected the trait had somehow been bred into the animals and passed on for generations in this supposedly gentle, calm, and placid friend of man. (Larry does not drink milk.)

The two of them are in complete agreement that the bane of their childhood years was a fighting rooster which Daddy kept around the barnyard for sentimental reasons as well as for purposes of reproduction. (Perhaps I should explain that cock fighting was against the law, but so was making whiskey and just because something was against the law was no great deterrent to hill folks. Almost all of Daddy's friends felt if God hadn't meant men to raise fighting roosters and drink corn whiskey, He would never have put the idea into their heads.)

Anyway, this ancient relic was a holdover from the period in Daddy's life when he enjoyed the fighting pit, and the old boy was allowed to run with the hens and enjoy existence as only a lone rooster in a henhouse can.

But my small siblings genuinely felt that this male domestic fowl's true purpose in life was to skulk around, lying in wait until he found them working in the garden, or hanging up clothes, or involved in other types of work which caused them to bend over and expose their back-sides. Sneaking up from behind like a thief in the night, he would hit with an explosion of feathers! Black and blue marks covered their thighs and behinds where the spur-like protuberances on the rooster's legs made direct contact with the soft portions of their slight bodies.

They deeply hated that pesky fowl and eventually came up with a plan of offensive action which worked pretty well. They carried an old worn-out broom with them when they were engaged in outside activities, and whenever their enemy came within striking distance they hit him as hard as they could. That was pretty hard.

One day Larry's aim was either extra good, or his blow was super powerful, because after receiving the blow, down the rooster dropped, graveyard dead! They did absolutely nothing to resurrect him, preferring Daddy's wrath to facing another few years at the mercy of that barnyard despot.

When they made their confession at supper over the chicken and dumplings provided by their long-time adversary, Daddy just grinned and said, "Well, kids, I'll bet the hens will miss him more than you will."

In all probability Daddy was right.

EPILOGUE

The book you have just read is true. The author, God knows, has taken great liberties but none of us would stand up in court and deny one word. It happened.

If you would like to know how we're all doing now, read on.

Kay Cash Sloan

Anne

First-born and favored by Mama and Daddy, Clive Anne is known to us as Sissy. She married Joe in 1941 and they celebrated their fiftieth anniversary this past spring. Joe has been in the family longer than some of the younger kids, and we think of him as "the wise old owl."

Joe's vivid stories of travels during WWII have left us with an understanding of what was really meant by the expression "War is hell!" On V.E. Day Joe, assigned to the prisoners guard unit, stayed near the radio shack. When the news of the war's end came through he called a young German who had been his translator many times and shared the great announcement. Before the young soldier told his comrades he threw his arms around his American friend and said, "Thank God, Joe. Now we can all be friends."

Joe's grandfather Frommel immigrated to the United States from Germany following the Civil War.

Clive tells of an early lesson in honesty she remembers

well. Daddy sent her to get change from the bank for his store and, when they counted it one penny too much turned up. She was promptly sent to return it. She asked for the bank president and said, "Your bank made a mistake and Daddy sent your penny back." The gentleman sat down, took the little girl on his knee, and for the first of many times one of Daddy's brood was told what a remarkable man we had for a father.

Clive is an avid collector of dolls and music boxes, antique and otherwise. She loves them all. She has always been our big sister, wiped tears, kept secrets, patched broken hearts and made that special dress we would have died without.

Clive and Joe have two children, Rebecca and Philip. Becky and her husband, Harold Cantrell, live in a lovely home that showcases a lifelong collection of antiques. They have a son, Steve, and daughter, Angie, who is married to Phillip Garrison, and they all live near one another.

Son Philip served eight years in the Air Force. He was wounded in action when he fell from the wing of a plane and broke his arm. "Stoney Lonesome," the old homeplace Joe's father built in 1916, was recently purchased by Philip and now it shelters him, his wife Kathy, son Robert, and daughter Tracy. That seems nice.

After thirty-nine years of "workin' on the road" Joe and Clive really enjoy retirement and are often found roaming over the Ozarks spending their kids inheritance.

Clark

The killer of the mule was Dan, or D. Boone, and he is a colorful character. When he was about five, Mama sent him to borrow vanilla flavoring from a neighbor. He smelled it, then tasted it and when Mama got the glass it was empty. At a tender age Dan developed his taste for spirits.

Dan remembers Christmas 1946, and he still reads from the leather book of poetry, his mother's Christmas gift to him, her young sailor far away from home.

Mama treasures Dan's gifts from foreign ports. I have a carving he brought me from Shanghai.

Since he was the first to leave home, Mama wrote him often. He will never forget the letter which carried the news that Old Pepper's replacement had kicked Daddy, breaking not only his jaw but also his brand new dentures. Dan cried.

Over the years Dan has made deer camp *the* place to be and many believe a fishing trip is not complete without D.

Boone.

Despite his circle of friends Dan remains a private person. A thinker and reader, over the years he has developed the philosophy he lives by...that of helping others. I have an example.

During the holiday season, not long ago, Dan won a bicycle. Early Christmas morning, way out in the country, a small boy was awakened by a phone call from "Santa," who said that in trying to get the bike down his chimney, he had made so much noise he frightened the reindeer and they all flew away. The boy found his gift just where "Santa" had left it...on his roof!

We believe Dan inherited from our maternal grandfather his love of woodworking. After his retirement from the railroad, he produced many items which are family treasures. Until his failing eyesight made continuing his hobby impossible, few could equal Dan in turning a piece of wood into a thing of beauty.

Daughter Dana Lee, and her husband, Lonnie Mills, live nearby with their sons, Alan and Andy. Their daughter, Alice, an honor student at a local college, recently tasted injustice and the papers were full. A heated debate raged between Alice and a prosecuting attorney. Such a public display of emotions might have been cause for concern in some circles.

Reverend Dennis Davis, Dan's stepson, remains a member of this family.

Martha

The author of this book has always been Fochie to the family and to her hometown friends. We don't know why. She was the smart one and it wasn't much fun having her for our sister. At school she completed assignments. At home it was even worse. She always wiped off the table and mopped in the corners. We sure were glad when she fell in love with Gene and went away.

After they got married and I came to know Gene, I prayed Fochie would die and I could have Gene. (Forget about Gregory Peck!) When they came home to visit they always piled us kids in their old yellow convertible and took us for a swim in the creek, and usually we stopped on the way home for a watermelon.

Patti was born in 1952 and life for the Bennetts hit the high road. They lived in Bloomfield, Missouri and their big, old white house was second home to us all. Some good memories were made there.

After retirement, the Bennetts relocated to south

Mississippi where they spend much time with Patti and her family. Patti is employment manager for a poultry production and processing company. She is in the M.B.A. program at the University of Southern Mississippi. She and her husband, Ken, enjoy the challenges and rewards of raising two teen-agers, Heather and Patrick.

Teasing Fochie is a family tradition, but we appreciate more than she guesses the talent, desire and determination that combine to make her our achiever. Our family is never surprised at what she does. We're just proud of her.

Bert

Bert, alias Linden Albert, L.A., or Lindy, is a legend. He holds records and friends seldom return from a hunting or fishing trip with L.A. sans a trophy.

If his fondest wish came true, Lindy would undergo cryonics the day following turkey season and be thawed just in time for the annual trek to Colorado. All the really big elk gather each fall when the word comes that L.A. is on his way. They draw straws and the short straw sacrifices self to the most feared of all bows.

Like Dan, Lindy sailored. He was in the shower in San Diego when his wallet was stolen and knowing he was to board a train soon for Florida, Lindy was worried. His mother heard the need in his voice (quite far removed from the usual teasing of "send me all your loose change") and in a Western Union station he soon laid eyes on his first one hundred dollar bill.

After leaving the Navy because it doesn't observe hunting season, Lindy married Barbara Hobbs. Of all the in-laws, and we've had fine ones, Bobbie has to be at the top of the list. She has put up with the Master of the Universe going on forty years. Not only himself and his off-spring, but the care of the bird dogs as well are all entrusted to her care.

Bobbie has raised good kids. Leslie, born just following Daddy's death, has always been the star on my Christmas tree. Now Mrs. John Pat McMurtry, she is mother of Neil and according to his "Paw" that's another book.

Son Patrick, taught by the "Master," also is an avid hunter. He and Cindy have two wonderful little girls, Stephanie and Nicole. Lindy calls them his "two Annas." No one knows why.

When my daughter underwent major surgery, thinking I could handle my problem best alone, I asked my family not to come with me. When Lindy walked into the waiting room I knew how wrong I'd been. His presence has sustained us more than once and to Jill and me there could never be anyone quite like Lindy.

Like several other family members, he has worked on the railroad all his adult life.

Recently the news carried the story of his involvement in the rescue of two people from Spring River. Somehow, this episode was no surprise to any of us who know Lindy. I guess all those years of slipping off to swim in the "sprang" paid off.

Reg

Reg is Darrel, or Deb to us all. Born a February child, he's different. He doesn't talk much, doesn't get excited, his wraths are rare but wicked. He's a survivor.

Most nights we crowded around the radio listening to Deb's selected programs; "The Lone Ranger," "Inner Sanctum," and "Amos and Andy." Deb didn't share controllership of the dial.

He served twenty years in the Air Force and saw from his window in the sky the mountains, deserts and oceans of this world. What to me would have been a dream come true was for Deb a day's work.

The time spent in Washington, D.C. with the military wing was memorable for him. He was privileged to meet dignitaries and heads of state from around the world.

Shortly before retirement, he married Bertha and she became "Bert" to us all. He inherited her large family and he survived.

On Valentine's Day, 1989, Deb repeated to us all his

doctor's report. End-stage heart disease. He needed a heart transplant. Without it, his chance of survival for one year was only forty percent.

Fate placed at Deb's bedside next day a miracle. The University Hospital stood ready to launch its heart transplant program. Systems "go," they had been waiting for a patient. After days of intensive and exhaustive testing, Deb's name was placed on the waiting list as that patient.

He needed his mate as few men ever do. She never faltered.

For months, Deb grew visibly weaker and our family closed ranks and waited. With one thought in mind we went about our lives and we waited.

When the phone rang Deb knew it was his call. The following evening he underwent surgery. Late in the night we knew great joy when we called Mama and Clive from the hospital to tell them Deb was going to be O.K. Mama cried.

We shared the sorrow of the donor's family who had lost someone they loved as much as we love Deb. We were humbled to receive the gift that came from hearts full of grief, yet still able to see another's suffering and care enough to want to ease the pain. There is little to say to those remarkable people. I believe they know what they have done and the love goes on.

Deb had been well prepared for the experience and his recovery exceeded his doctor's expectations. Today life is pretty much back to normal. He works every day and he does like to fish, but like the rest of us he receives his daily blessings with a richer understanding.

Leah

Our youngest sister, Leah, is really Linda, who grew to become Ginna. No one knows where our extra names come from. They are just here...they have always been here.

She married early and Bill allowed her to remain a wife and mother. She abundantly enjoyed that life. Then one day the kids grew up.

Suffering more than most from the empty nest syndrome, she complained bitterly of life passing her by. Recently joining and conquering quickly the working world, she decided (as I had told her) that bed *is* better at 5:00 AM. Ginna took early retirement.

Now feeling more satisfied, Ginna keeps busy doing what she does best. She keeps track of us. When we need news of Mama or anything else, it is Ginna's phone that rings.

Her home reflects her talent. Handmade rugs cover hardwood floors. The breeze tickles crocheted curtains.

Pickles in the pantry - fried pies on the porch. A late night raid on the Crase refrigerator reveals real food, scratch food.

Sisters could not have lived more different lives, but we share a heart and have never been afraid to expose our deepest selves to one another.

While Ginna was in the dog raising business, I suffered one of my crises and wanted to talk. I found her all bundled up out by the dog pens and never was she happier to see me. I soon knew why. Her dogs had been exposed to some exotic disease and my crisis was put on hold while we gave shots to twenty-three squirming cocker spaniels.

Michael, Jessie, Cole and Courtney have a gingerbread baking, paper doll playing granny like most children only read about, and they are always the source of her greatest joy.

The news director and well-known local d.j. is her son. Mike loves his kids, Nina, sports, and the woods.

Robin followed her brother into broadcasting and, now divorced, she quite successfully juggles her jobs; news director, announcer, and mother. One must walk in her shoes to know it is not as easy as Robin makes it look.

Ginna gives Bill a measure of credit for his part in all this. On a scale of one to ten, as brothers-in-law go, Bill is a fourteen and a half.

To me they are the family of choice. On chilly evenings a fire burns, and it's good to be at Ginna's at suppertime.

Larry

The baby boy in our family, Larry John, has always delighted in signing his legal documents "Johnny Cash." It's permissible and like the rest of us Johnny enjoys a good commotion. Imagine the one that started the night word spread through the hospital halls that Johnny Cash's wife was in the labor room.

Johnny spent some time with us in California when Jill was a tiny baby and one evening she started acting even funnier than usual. After discovering what had happened, my pediatrician begged me not to panic and promised that Jill would live. (I had called him as soon as I'd paid Johnny for the entire pack of his cigarettes she had eaten!)

I moved home to Missouri before my husband did. Johnny followed in a month or so, and my house was his first stop. Greeted by Ginna and me screaming, "Oh, Johnny, kill it! There's a mouse in the toilet!" Johnny knew he was home.

He married Lou in the first church wedding any of us

had. And it worked. Still together and with the same job after all these years, they live in their new home built on several acres near Six Flags Over Mid-America.

His daughter, Vicki, her husband, Roger, and their new baby, Brian Joseph, are close enough for Grandpa and Grandma to enjoy.

Johnny's other reason for living is his cars. He races with some success throughout the area. One night in Cape Girardeau I was a witness. He had left me in an awful place to wait. It was hot, smelly, smokey and quite horrible. A friend finally let me in on the joke. Johnny had left me in the pit. On the bleachers with other spectators, I enjoyed a thrilling night.

Johnny is proud to show off his well-stocked garage which he keeps as neat as a pin. It contains almost anything needed to maintain vehicles and his many friends know they are welcome to use any or all of the tools. Just put them back in the right place. Johnny is particular about that.

Mama's room often contains fresh flowers sent by one of her kids who remembers.

Mama

In December of 1955 Daddy died and life changed forever. The years following were almost unbearable for Mama but her faith allowed her to again put us first. She struggled to maintain a home for us all, but most especially for Johnny and Linda who were still small.

Clive and Joe became her mainstays at this time and emotional and financial support from them was the norm.

In 1959 Mama and Johnny moved to town to be near her new job as cook at the school cafeteria. Mama always walked to work and speaks with justifiable pride of never missing a day of work. Only once in her five year career did the ice get so bad that she had to resort to a taxi.

Good Mama made her home with Mama after Good Papa died and we fondly remember that angel.

The last Christmas dinner Mama cooked for us was memorable. She insisted we trim the guest list to the immediate family for her small apartment offered little room. God smiled on Mama and about forty of us ate on

165

picnic tables in the yard with the temperature an un-believable 72 degrees.

She has enjoyed good health, mental and physical. Even her first trip to the hospital at age 79 was great.

Serious was the fractured pelvis she received in a fall and the painful recovery was hard even for this lady. To please her kids, Mama gave up her apartment and moved into a boarding home. We all sleep better knowing she is never alone.

Her biggest problem now is failing eyesight, and that is slowly improving following cataract surgery. Once again she is crocheting those beautiful rag rugs.

When I asked Mama if she'd like to add anything to the book she answered, "Yes, Kay, I would. I'd like to say that I must have done something right to have raised the bunch of kids that I did and have them turn out as well as they have."

Mama loves us.

Iris

Really I'm Kay and I still don't eat slimy things.

Born with a restless spirit, I have roamed more than the others. An enigma even to me, I poured myself into various molds but was never comfortable.

My prayers were answered when Jill was born and one Christmas Eve I brought my little girl home to Fochie's.

Soon after, I entered college and my term paper, "How My Husband Influenced My Decision to Obtain a Writ of Divorcement," added much to my reputation as a nut. Though the marriage had failed, my paper got an A+.

Two years later I was among those listed cum laude in my nursing graduation class. Could be some brains with the bull.

Jill and I lived an adventure. She loved everything alive and in nursing I had found my niche. Studying for state boards one night, I reached for a cigarette and picked up her pet snake. I really love Jill a lot!

The Kern River has played forever in California's Sierra

Mountains. In the tiny town of Kernville Jill lives with her husband, John Seals, and my granddaughter, Nicole. The river offers these white water nuts a life style most would envy.

Jill was happy to illustrate the book you have just read. In addition to working regular jobs, she and her husband manufacture "Seals Spray Skirts." That's kayak stuff.

Mid-life holds no crises for me but rather the contentment I found several years ago when the ol' cowboy, Bill Reece, introduced me to his Appaloosas and his love for playing Blue Grass music. The shack, as we refer to our home built by the hands of our good friends, the Hills, welcomes a wide variety of companions to the table Dan made.

In his last months when Daddy knew he was very ill, he often teased Mama with, "I'm comin' back, you know, God willin', after the first hard freeze in the fall and I'll be out there listenin' to my dogs run."

Some of us believe if the Great God Almighty can allow, Daddy's spirit walks the woods. On frosty November nights he's out there listening to the hounds.

Like the hills, our family endures. We bury our loved ones and we survive our broken marriages. The years find us closer, with deepening bonds and a greater concern for each other.

With spirits that soar and stumble, we conquer and we accept defeat. We thrill to darkness and each snowfall. When our numbers lessen we will close ranks, draw deeply from the well within and endure, secure in the knowledge that Mama and Daddy will wait for us and we will be home by suppertime.

—Kay Cash Sloan
Poplar Bluff, MO (1991)

Mama
1922

Anne, Daddy, Martha, Clark
1933

Martha, Reg, Iris, Bert, Billy Waddles
1940

Reg and Iris
1941

Mama and Daddy
1949

Mama Cash
1950

Clark and Anne
1929

Clark, Bert, Martha, Reg, Anne
1938

Larry
1951

Anne and Granma Bryan
Mama and Goodmama
1924

Daddy
1940

Leah
1954

Martha
1931